LOVE YOU,

HATE THE PORN

LOVE YOU,

HATE THE PORN

*Healing a Relationship Damaged
by Virtual Infidelity*

MARK CHAMBERLAIN, PhD
GEOFF STEURER, MS, LMFT

SHADOW
MOUNTAIN

SALT LAKE CITY, UTAH

Visit us at ShadowMountain.com

Library of Congress Cataloging-in-Publication Data

Chamberlain, Mark D. (Mark David), 1964– author.
  Love you, hate the porn : healing a relationship damaged by virtual infidelity / Mark Chamberlain, PhD ; Geoff Steurer, MS, LMFT.
      pages   cm
  Includes bibliographical references and index.
  ISBN 978-1-60641-936-6 (paperbound)
  1. Pornography.   2. Sex addiction.   I. Steurer, Geoff, 1974– author.   II. Title.
HQ471.C43 2011

362.196'85833—dc22   2010048772

Printed in the United States of America
Alexander's Print Advantage

10   9   8

CONTENTS

INTRODUCTION

It may be cybersex, but it can feel like real infidelity to your partner. There's nothing virtual about the damage pornography does to a relationship. Porn can keep the two of you from feeling close and connected, interfering with your ability to meet your most important needs in your most important relationship. When you're hooked on porn, the wounds are reopened each time a relapse is discovered. Even when you keep your commitment to stay away from porn, your marriage may continue to suffer. As tough as it is to overcome a porn habit, healing a marriage damaged by porn is even harder. It can get so bad for some couples that they separate and divorce. Others stay together, but the strain of unresolved feelings takes a distinct, if not always acknowledged toll.

If you're the one who's hurting because of your partner's pornography habit, it's not enough for your loved one to simply stop looking at porn. You need healing yourself. Whether you keep bringing it up or suffer silently, emotional wounds can fester, fueling fights about other things and causing disconnected feelings.

Many couples begin to wonder, "Can our marriage heal? Will we ever feel close again?"

Your marriage can help heal a pornography habit—even one that's deteriorated into a full-blown addiction. Here's why: the pleasure of pornography is fleeting, and no genuine human need is filled by its consumption. By contrast, feeling emotionally close as a couple satisfies people in a deep, sustaining way. This attachment meets a universal need that defines our very essence as a species. We humans are, as biologists put it, "pair bonders." Our souls hunger for the kind of special, exclusive, and lasting sense of connection that only a strong marriage can bring. We are more complete as couples. While pornography strikes at the heart of this attachment, healing together can reestablish and even deepen the bond.

Recovery has three different aspects, *his, hers,* and *ours.* In this book, we've chosen not to delve deeply into spiritual aspects of recovery, therapeutic solutions, or individual efforts. We focus on what you can do together as a couple—and there is a lot that can be done. The topic has become a passion for us because we've seen so many people work hard and do well in their efforts to heal as individuals, only to have their relationship continue to flounder.

We've found no better road map for the path of couples' healing than Sue Johnson's Emotionally Focused Couples Therapy. Her work at the University of Ottawa has developed into the most effective and research-validated way to treat couples in distress. We've seen this perspective help many couples and we're excited to share it with you.

Despite how important your relationship is, please make no mistake: as you strive to overcome the damage pornography has done, some of the work you'll do must be done on your own. For instance, no matter how much work a couple does together to heal their marriage, what if a wife senses that her husband is half-hearted in his efforts to avoid pornography when he's alone? She'll likely doubt his emotional availability and find herself unable to invest wholeheartedly in building a stronger bond with him. If you find that the process of healing together derails even when you're giving it your all, ask yourself if you or your partner has more individual, foundational work to do before the relationship can feel secure enough for the two of you to start growing together again. (For more on key ingredients of his and her individual recoveries, please see our website: hatetheporn.com.)

Whatever it takes, don't give up! Your individual healing is worth it. And then, as you heal your relationship as well, you will reap some of the greatest rewards life has to offer.

CHAPTER 1

A CANCER THAT CAN RAVAGE RELATIONSHIPS

Throughout her life, Sally had never objected to pornography on moral grounds. She'd always figured it was up to individuals to decide for themselves what they did for entertainment. Recently, however, she'd been developing an objection of a different sort. Rather than moral, it was visceral.

It spread from a sick feeling in her stomach up to a choking heaviness in her chest. It had started several months ago when she'd discovered at three in the morning that she was alone in bed. She'd gotten up to look for Lyle and found him downstairs pausing the DVR and rewinding it again and again to watch a sex scene. She'd stood there in shock, that awful feeling coming in waves up her torso, as she realized that her husband was, in his mind, having sex with that stranger on the screen. She was even more troubled by the fact that he hadn't even heard her behind him. He never noticed her standing there until she said something to him.

Obviously, he had been in another world. But even worse, he seemed different. She had the terrifying feeling that this was somehow not the man she thought she'd married. "Do I even know you?" she had asked him. "*Really* know you?"

Lyle had insisted that he'd had no idea how strongly she would react to what he was viewing, that porn meant nothing to him, and that he would gladly and easily avoid it in the future now that he knew how she felt about it. Lyle hadn't realized how Sally would react, and frankly, neither had she. She was embarrassed that it bothered her so much.

Sally knew what kind of guy Lyle was deep down. After all, she'd watched him with his kids. He was patient with her dogs, who could be a real pain. She'd knelt beside him, handing him tools, on the floor of their elderly neighbor's bathroom as he repaired her toilet. She'd chosen him because he was a great guy, she kept reminding herself. She wanted to be able to be less bothered by that incident, to get over it and move on in their relationship.

Nonetheless, it had taken Sally a couple of months to sleep soundly through the night again. And her chiropractor was still working on the knot he couldn't seem to knead out of the base of her neck. Even worse, she no longer threw on sweats in the evening when they both got home from work. She'd added more sit-ups to her workout routine to try to tighten up her abs. She'd even caught herself checking her makeup in the bathroom mirror at nine o'clock at night. *What's gotten into me?* she wondered. Rather than enjoying her time with Lyle, she felt like she was performing in an effort to hold his interest. She finally admitted to herself that she now felt locked in a potential contest between her and every porn actress out there for his attention and affection. She might have beaten back the first wave of attack—he was still here with her—but eventual defeat seemed inevitable. *After all, just look at me,* she would think when she looked at herself in the mirror. She had felt fine about her body a few months ago, but now all she could see was a bundle of flaws. Most disappointing to Sally was the realization that she was more relaxed and felt freer to be herself when she and Lyle were in different rooms of the house. There'd been no horseplay or wrestling or lighthearted teasing for months now.

She felt less secure in their relationship. When Lyle went to a college buddy's bachelor party, she wondered whether she could trust him. When they were out in public, he seemed focused on the bodies of attractive women. She kept watching him surf through the channels until he found something titillating, and she saw how entranced he got when a sexy or scantily clothed girl came on-screen.

Lyle could tell that Sally was different now, and he kept asking her if she was okay. When she would leave their bedroom at night, he'd eventually come find her and try to talk with her. At first she hardly knew what to ask him for. She didn't want to be absurd. He wanted to feel close to her again and he kept trying to comfort her, but it felt now to him like she had retreated into a shell.

Finally, when Lyle kept asking and asking what was wrong and if there was anything he could do to help her feel secure again, she acknowledged to him just how deeply she was being affected. "When I think you're lusting after other women, it rocks me to the core. I get scared that I'm going to lose you to someone else. I can't take that. You know how much you matter to me. I can't bear that thought. So I have to get some distance between us. I know it sounds crazy, but I pull away to protect myself. When I get so sick inside, I don't have a choice. It's better to be apart at those times than to try to be close to you when I know what I'd be competing with."

Sally felt bad that her insecurities had come between them like this. However, it also felt good that Lyle had persisted in asking her what was wrong, which had convinced her that he really wanted to hear it. Now, having revealed everything, she stood emotionally naked in front of Lyle.

Lyle sat, pondering everything Sally had said. She could tell by the look on his face that he took her feelings seriously. He didn't seem to think that she was being silly at all. What a tremendous relief.

"Hon," Lyle finally responded, "we obviously have different reactions to erotic entertainment. After that first incident in the middle of the night I should have gotten it, but I'm a slow learner, I guess. Talking about it again tonight, it's really sinking in for me how much this hurts you, and that's the last thing I want. Thanks for not giving up on me. I can see that I need to respect your sensibilities more. I am going to work on it, I promise. I want nothing more than for us to have back the comfort and ease that we used to have with each other." Lyle walked over, sat next to Sally, took her hand in his, and kissed her on the forehead.

Sally had never shared with anyone her feelings the way she just had with Lyle. She'd been telling herself that she was overreacting, so to have Lyle want to know what was going on inside for her and then commit to honor her feelings was such a relief. "Thank you," she sighed. "I don't want this to come between us anymore. I don't want *anything* to come between us."

This was just the beginning for Sally and Lyle, but at least the needed change was beginning to happen. Reaching out, understanding, and connection were taking the place of misunderstanding and separateness.

SURVEYING THE DAMAGE

The harm pornography does to relationships has been quantified and measured. Indiana University researchers Dolf Zillman and Jennings Bryant had research subjects view porn for six weeks; they then compared the subjects' attitude ratings from before and after. These subjects became less satisfied with their real-life sexual partners, saw monogamy as less desirable and faithfulness to one's spouse as less important, and were more prone to overestimate the prevalence of less common sexual practices such as group sex, bestiality, and sadomasochistic activity. They even came to perceive victims of sex crimes as suffering less and being less severely wronged. Perhaps most troubling in the context of our discussion, after viewing that amount of pornography, these subjects became more cynical in their attitudes about love and more accepting of the idea that superior sexual satisfaction is attainable without having affection for one's partner. They were more prone to see marriage as sexually confining and to view raising children and having a family as an unattractive prospect. Since the time of the initial study in the 1970s, these results have been replicated in similar studies (Zillman and Bryant 1988).

As disturbing as these statistically measurable changes in attitude may be, it's even more chilling to see the effects of pornography in real life. Documentary filmmaker Lance Tracy followed one couple who volunteered for the husband to go through the same experience as the subjects in Zillmann and Bryant's experiments: six weeks of daily pornography consumption. When we're introduced to the couple, Debbie and Josh, early in the film, the rapport they share is obvious by their eye contact and the way they joke with each other. Fast-forward to the follow-up interview seven weeks later, and things between them appear to have taken a distinct downturn. Perhaps most surprising, Josh doesn't think that his attitudes or relationship have been affected by the pornography. The sincerity is apparent in his eyes as he says so to Mr. Tracy. As he's talking, the changes in his ratings flash on-screen, and they're the very same differences Zillmann and Bryant identified in the studies described above.

Among other changes noted, Josh trusted Debbie less. That's

right: The partner viewing the pornography had less faith in his wife's commitment and fidelity. Both Josh and Debbie were less satisfied with each other and their relationship. They had less confidence that they would continue in the future as a couple. The film's director felt so bad about this outcome that he arranged and paid for couples therapy to help this couple try to repair the rift that had developed between them (Tracy, "Adult Entertainment").

Spouses of those who view pornography compulsively don't need social scientists or documentary filmmakers to convince them their relationships are being eroded. In one study, the complaints of women who perceived their husbands to be heavily involved in pornography were analyzed, and two dominant themes emerged: First, they observed that their husbands had a decreased sexual desire for them. Second, when they did have sex, the way they were treated left them feeling more like a sex object than a lover, or even a person (Bergner and Bridges 2002).

The wife of one of my clients disclosed to him more than a year after he was porn-free, "At times I haven't enjoyed sex with you. Sometimes it felt like you didn't need me because you were getting satisfaction elsewhere. At other times it felt like you were coming to me just for the sex, not out of interest in me. Instead of being an expression of the connection between us, it seemed more mechanical. Then, when you denied that you were back into the porn and yet it felt that way again, I wondered what was wrong with *me*. It was enough to make me think I was going crazy!" As his wife was wondering what was wrong with her, why didn't my client recognize her struggle and come to her aid more quickly? Gail Dines, author of *Pornland: How Porn Has Hijacked Our Sexuality,* commented that one of pornography's most destructive effects is that it "trains men to become desensitized to women's pain" (Dines 2010, 74).

The Worst Wound

Pornography can afflict a couple's relationship the way a malignant cancer ravages a body. The most devastating thing pornography does is come between a man and woman at the worst times and in the worst way. Right at those moments when a person is struggling and in need emotionally, pornography offers an alternative—a relationship counterfeit. Pornography becomes something that person can go to for soothing and an illusory sense of connection and vitality. And that, perhaps, is pornography's real virulence, its ultimate price: When he's going to *it,* he's not going to *her.*

A client recently said to me, "I don't go to porn when I'm feeling a sexual desire that hasn't been satisfied. I go to my wife, Ally, for that. It's when we are struggling as a couple, and I lose hope of being happy together and having a good relationship. That's when I take that path. When things are going well between me and Ally, it's like I'm invincible to the urges." This is often a shocking revelation to most people affected by the impact of pornography. They have assumed that it was only about out-of-control sexual urges. In reality, the pull of pornography results more from unmanaged emotional and relationship pain. Think of it as attempting to meet healthy needs in unhealthy ways.

When we're feeling raw or emotionally vulnerable, it's as though the lid is off the emotional superglue for us. We're primed and ready to bond. We gravitate to things we hope might soothe us, and our nervous system prepares us to connect in a powerful way to whatever it is that "works" to comfort, satisfy, or distract. Having experienced in the past this kind of binding event in a time of need, in the future our minds are likely to recall what we went to for soothing and gravitate back to it when we're in need.

We are hardwired from birth to seek comfort when we feel distress or pain. This reflex to reach toward soothing happens faster than we can even logically recognize it. It takes about 100 milliseconds for our brain to react emotionally in this way, and yet about 600 milliseconds for our thinking brain, our cortex, to register the reaction. These lightning-quick, subconscious longings for relief and comfort automatically orient us toward activities we've experienced as soothing. As a result, our inclinations in such moments of need may result more from conditioning than from choice.

You may, for example, turn on the radio and listen to music. If that doesn't quite do the trick and you still feel out of sorts, then you're still emotionally thirsty, and the hunt for a quencher continues. The lid is still off the emotional superglue. Let's say you then zone out in front of the TV for a while. You may keep sitting and watching, engaged to some degree, an apparent indicator that you might be getting some kind of satisfaction or relief from the process. However, a couple of hours later, when you think about turning it off and turning your attention back to your life, that unsettled, uneasy feeling is sitting right there, waiting. You decide not to hit the power button just yet. Before long, your spouse has gone to bed. The house is silent—everyone but you is sleeping. You're still surfing the channels. You don't feel relaxed enough to sleep. You're not yet wound down. There remains some lingering emotional energy—stirred up, pent up. You still need a release. Your system is still seeking comfort and soothing. The lid is still off the emotional superglue.

Channel after channel after channel after channel, you circle around and around again. There are some titillating advertisements. You start to feel different, more focused and alive. Then you run on to a salacious program. Your attention is riveted. The seduction builds to a sex scene, followed by minimal plot material and then another sex scene. You are in a different world now. The emotional landscape has morphed and you are completely free of the unsettled feeling that was haunting you. You may have other thoughts pestering you, like neon signs along the side of the road, trying to break into your consciousness. Thoughts about how it's the middle of the night and you really should be sleeping so that you can function more effectively the next day. Thoughts about how you were intending to give up this habit of seeking, viewing, and then masturbating to sexual content on TV and the Internet. But those thoughts don't stop you now. Once that program is over, you retreat to the bathroom and lock the door. Afterward, you try not to think about anything. Mercifully, your mind remains blank, your inner arousal level finally settling to match the quiet all around you in your home. The emotional and bodily relief is real, even though it's not the deep comfort you crave. The emptiness may feel a bit yucky, but at least the emotionally jagged feelings have been blunted. You know from experience that tomorrow the guilt about what you've just done will creep in, but sleep comes quickly at this point, delivering you from consciousness.

So what happened with the emotional superglue? You did not realize it at the time—or even recognize later what happened—but you certainly experienced the results. You were feeling emotionally raw, and something helped you restore an inner sense of equilibrium. Having had that experience, you are now more emotionally attached to whatever that was. Unfortunately, it was pornography and masturbation. Even more regrettably, it was not opening up to your wife and making an emotional connection to her. It could have been her. It should have been her. But there is a block in your ability or willingness to go to her when you're in need emotionally.

For many of us, our failure to seek emotional relief within our most important relationship results not only from a lack of ability but also from an ignorance or lack of awareness. We simply may not recognize those initial stirrings, those uneasy feelings as indicators of our need for emotional connection and relationship soothing. And thus we become sitting ducks, much more vulnerable to the pull and hold of pornography.

The Damage Deepens

Things will be different after a night like the one just described. The fleeting benefits of porn give way to lingering costs. First, there are physical effects. You're sleep deprived and exhausted, of course, but there's even more. Oxytocin is a hormone that calms the nervous system, soothes us emotionally, and helps bond us to our sexual partner. This chemical is most famous for its role in bonding infants to their mothers, since it is released during breastfeeding. However, it is also released in both men and women when we touch, hold, and caress one another. Affectionately known as the "cuddle chemical," oxytocin is released in abundance after sexual climax. However, researchers have measured a relative void of oxytocin in the bloodstream of individuals who engaged in sex without a partner—those who masturbated to pornography. To be exact, those who had intercourse with their beloved were shown to have 400 percent more oxytocin in their bloodstream. The afterglow of sex with a partner contrasts sharply with the oxytocin-depleted emptiness that follows consumption of porn (Brody and Kroger 2006).

Pornography can be like a drug in its effects, and, like any other addictive drug, it leaves us worse off than it found us. Physically and emotionally, you will likely end up more needy after such a night than you were before. You will be in withdrawal, experiencing the low that always follows a druglike high. This is how tolerance develops—the need to take more of a drug in order to experience the same effect. You want to feel better the next day, too, but now you have further to go in order to feel okay since your experience the day before took you down a few notches. Your body has adjusted to intensity by dampening its response. Your pleasure and contentment chemicals are more depleted than before. Equilibrium will be harder to restore.

Not only are you more in need emotionally, but the best avenue for successfully meeting those needs—your marriage—is even more blocked than it was yesterday. Even if you've tried to convince yourself that this behavior had nothing to do with your wife or your relationship with her, masturbating to pornography has unavoidably affected your marriage. The next morning, you'll feel sheepish at least, get-me-out-of-her-presence ashamed at worst. You'll be less likely to look her in the eyes. The next time you would benefit from emotional connection and relationship soothing, you'll be less able to reach out to her. You'll feel more like dealing with it on your own. And porn will be right there waiting for you. Not as effective, perhaps, as connecting with her, but seemingly safe and certainly less risky emotionally.

For too many, unfortunately, this pattern continues on and on. In everyday life, distressing emotions are always going to keep getting stirred up, leaving us primed and in need of something. As much as we may want to kick the porn habit and turn our lives around, continuing the same course is the path of least resistance.

One of the reasons pornography draws people in and keeps them hooked is that it offers physical and emotional soothing in a way that doesn't require as much emotional risk as reaching out to a partner would. Opening up about something in their lives that's painful, disappointing, intimidating, or downright scary is difficult and frightening. And yet the reflex to seek human comfort when emotionally distressed is, as we said, hardwired into every human. Pornography can mimic the experience of being comforted by a loving attachment figure in that it activates some of the same physiological soothing mechanisms. Plus, it's always available, easy to access, doesn't require us to be vulnerable, and consistently delivers the desired relief. Of course, the relief too quickly gives way to feelings of shame and guilt, sometimes even self-loathing.

By the time this cycle has gone on in your life for months or years, your appraisal of yourself can be pretty low. It may seem impossible to change. "How could I ever go to her when I'm in need? This huge secret is now a wedge between us, and I can't talk to her about the porn. If she really knew that it's been such a big problem for me, she could never accept and love me. In fact, she might just leave me over it."

The habit is well ingrained and the walls on both sides of the canyon are steep. Every time you struggle emotionally, the lid comes off the emotional superglue once again. Every time you go to pornography, you miss out on the emotional soothing that you could be receiving from your wife. You become more and more attached—bonded, dependent, reliant, and perhaps even addicted—to the pornography habit you're trying to give up. And all the time you feel less worthy of your wife's love and less able to go to her about your porn problem or anything else you're struggling with.

It's a difficult dilemma: The more you seek out pornography, the more isolated and distressed you become. Your need for real human connection with your wife increases, and yet your ability to go to her for it decreases. You pull away more in secrecy and shame, and the cycle of disconnection from yourself and from her continues.

THE POWER OF DRAWING TOGETHER

Once a pornography problem is revealed, either through voluntary disclosure or a spouse's discovery, the destructive cycle of isolation and addiction can be interrupted. The partners can start to draw together instead of allowing their relationship to continue to be torn apart. She can share with him the distress she has felt over the disconnection that pornography has created or perpetuated. He can learn to recognize when he's feeling bad and in need of support and develop the habit of going to her at such times.

This is not to say that they will immediately find bliss as a couple. The skill of seeking soothing within the relationship and the process of developing emotional connection are complex and challenging. Spouses take tremendous emotional risks when they move toward each other during such a relational crisis. He feels ashamed and worthless in her eyes. When he reaches out anyway, it's an act of tremendous courage, one to be admired even when it doesn't turn out ideally because she's still hurting so badly. Remember, she's been feeling betrayed and unloved.

The movements partners make toward each other are often slow and cautious. Drawing together in this way won't bring the kind of instant gratification and relief pornography promises. Nonetheless, when couples stick with it, the process can work for both partners. Everyday distresses and needs aren't as problematic as when they drove disconnection and addiction. In fact, they become opportunities for bonding. When emotional arousal is triggered, the lid still comes off the emotional superglue. However, as couples seek each other out, draw together in such key moments, and feel better for having faced a difficult emotion together, their bond deepens and becomes a more and more profound connection over time. They stick together until they're stuck together in a way that permits nothing to come between them.

This is the kind of relationship a couple can develop even after a pornography problem has done its damage. I've seen many couples do it. The rest of the book is about how they've achieved it—and how you can too!

Questions to Consider and Discuss

Some couples wonder if pornography is a problem for them. The following questions can help you determine if pornography is negatively affecting your relationship.

- Do we have open disagreements or unspoken differences when it comes to sexually oriented media?
- Has the use of the Internet become a problem in our relationship?
- Has sex become a wedge or divisive topic between us instead of something that helps us feel close and connected?
- Has one of us engaged in behavior while online that has offended the other (or would offend that person if he or she knew about it)?
- Does one of us seem to the other to be overly fascinated or involved with sexually explicit or suggestive videos, pictures, writing, or interacting?
- Has one partner's behavior along these lines led to underlying tension or outright arguments?
- Has one partner's involvement with pornography or other sexual behavior negatively affected his or her relationships, spirituality, career, emotional well-being, or our finances?
- Does either of us find that his or her emotional energy is drained by suspicions, premonitions, hunches, worries, or anxieties that pornography or other sexual involvements play a larger role in the other's life than he or she reveals?
- Has pornography led one of us to feel less secure that the other remains sexually faithful now, or to feel less confident in his or her future fidelity?

CHAPTER 2

WE'RE BOTH WORKING, BUT IT'S NOT WORKING

B efore we talk about how you can heal your relationship, it's important to understand why initial efforts at healing so often fail. We've discovered over the years that problems can fester even when both husband and wife demonstrate a high commitment level and exert a lot of energy trying to work through a pornography problem. Too often, despite how much they both care and invest, their relationship continues to flounder. This usually happens when spouses keep getting into a negative cycle in the way they deal with issues related to pornography.

A NEGATIVE CYCLE IN ACTION

Craig and Cheryl are walking through the mall. Things have been good for the last couple of days, and that's a relief to both of them, a much-needed break. The tension and conflict has been at such a high level between them. It all started at that moment three weeks ago when Cheryl walked in and caught Craig viewing pornography on his cell phone when he was supposed to be taking care of their three kids. It has been hellish for much of the time since then . . . but now, for a change, it's almost as though they're like any other couple walking through the mall. They could almost forget that this problem has done such damage to their relationship and looms over them still like a dark cloud.

Almost.

Craig spots it first: a gigantic photo advertisement of a woman in lingerie up ahead on their right. Cheryl sees it and glances at Craig, who quickly glances back and sees that she sees that he was looking at it. He then sees her eyes narrow and her head cock in a rebuking gesture, and he knows what she's thinking: *Really, Craig? After everything we've been through?*

Craig's eyes widen, as if pleading, *What did I do? I swear I just noticed it. I wasn't ogling, I just glanced. It was just a fraction of a second, for crying out loud!*

Cheryl sighs, exasperated.

Craig rolls his eyes, just as exasperated.

Cheryl's stride is now brisk and stiff. She's hurting, but the hurt quickly converts to anger. Craig marches to keep up, feeling like a scolded puppy, ashamed . . . but quickly moving into resentment over the fact that he can't seem to do anything right in her eyes.

His perversion and deception have left my life in ruins, Cheryl thinks. *I was already struggling to feel good about my body, and now I discover he's looking at that crap! How can I stay with a man who would put me through this? What does that say about me as a woman? Am I really going to live in this kind of relationship? Can I really be that much of a doormat? And look at him! He's defensive when I bring it up. He minimizes it instead of being more attentive and reassuring. And yet other people think he's such a compassionate, caring person. All of that's just a façade, and look at the real*

WE'RE BOTH WORKING, BUT IT'S NOT WORKING

man that I get: can't even control his lust when he's holding hands with his wife.

Meanwhile, Craig concludes, *It's hopeless. No matter what I do to try to make this better, none of it ever gets through to her. She's convinced that I'm a jerk, convinced that I want other women instead of her, and convinced that I'm unsuitable as husband material. Back when it was a secret, I just knew that if she found out about my pornography struggles, she'd never be able to forgive me for it. Her whole family's this way: judgmental and self-righteous. I have never been good enough in their eyes, or in hers. If our marriage ends, maybe it will be for the best.*

THE LEGITIMATE NEEDS THAT FUEL NEGATIVE CYCLES

Men's and women's most pressing relationship needs are often different, and that can really wreak havoc as they interact about the hot-button issue of pornography. For instance, husbands often have a very pressing need for *acceptance* from their wives. They so deeply want to get along, to feel like there's peace in the relationship and that things are smooth between them as a couple. A man feels loved and confident when he knows that his wife is pleased and contented.

The wife, by contrast, typically has an equally pressing need to maintain a sense of *closeness* with her husband. She so deeply wants to know what's happening inside for him, to talk about how things are going. She wants to make sure that their hearts and minds are on the same page and that they're working together on issues and problems.

It may not seem like a big difficulty, this gap or variance between what each of them yearns for most out of the relationship. However, each partner's need is, to him or her, like emotional oxygen. If they're not getting it, they can become panicky and fixated. Neither can give what the other needs because they're both now scrambling so desperately for what they need. Feeling so unacceptable in Cheryl's eyes, Craig can't draw close to her. So distraught that she may never have the closeness she needs, Cheryl literally cannot convey approval and acceptance. Each partner becomes even more distraught and fixated as the cycle escalates. Watch how it can affect their interaction:

A couple of weeks after the problem in the mall, Cheryl wants to talk as they finally collapse into bed one night. "How did things go for you today?" she says.

"Fine."

"I mean with temptation."

"It was fine," Craig said. "I've told you I have no desire for that stuff since it's all come out in the open. Today was the same as yesterday, and the same as the time before that when you asked. It will probably be going fine if you ask tomorrow. I realize that because of my behavior you have every right to ask, but it seems like you're not convinced even if I tell you things are going well."

Craig desperately craves a restored sense that there is peace between them again, a feeling of acceptance from her. But remember, she needs to feel the closeness that comes from intimate involvement in the intricacies of his life. She wants to keep her finger on his emotional pulse.

"I've been reading about pornography addiction," Cheryl says, "and they say that almost all men relapse several times along the way in their recovery. You're telling me you're unique, and that it's just suddenly over for you?"

"I don't know how many times I have to tell you: It was a relief to get it out in the open," Craig counters. "I hated keeping the secret and living a double life. I'm *happy* you know. It makes it easier. It's *easy* now. I'm just trying to tell you the truth. Should I lie and say that I'm struggling just to make you feel better? Even when I was having the problem, sometimes I'd go weeks or even months without giving in. It wasn't ever as big of a deal as you seem to think it is. I think that all your reading is actually making this worse in your mind."

Again we see it: He wants there to be peace between them again; she's looking for connection by way of opennness and involvement.

"So now I'm exaggerating your problem and making things worse by learning about it. Amazing! I guess I was mistaken to think that you might be grateful for the help. I know, I know, I should just stop bugging you and everything would be fine. Well, things aren't fine! I've been devastated! I think about it all the time now, Craig! You think I like thinking about this stuff?! I hate it! And I'm starting to hate you for ruining what I *thought* we had together!"

"Cheryl, if you only knew how common this is. Most men aren't even trying to stop! It's not like I'm some pervert. I'm still the same guy you thought I was, I just had this struggle you didn't know about. It doesn't make me some terrible person!"

"You're the same guy I thought I was married to, with only one small difference: You're a guy who looks at pictures of other women and fantasizes about having sex with them. Oh yeah, and you're a guy who could keep a habit like this a secret from the woman he's married to for seven years. That's all. Just those two little differences."

"I'm not going to talk to you if you're going to be sarcastic." Craig throws back the covers and gets up out of bed.

"Go ahead and leave," Cheryl shouts through sobs. "That's what you always do! You won't even stay here and work through it with me! Once again I have to deal with the tough stuff on my own!"

"You're going to wake up the kids!" Craig retorts through gritted teeth.

"The kids?" Cheryl shouts after him as he leaves the room. "You're concerned about the *kids?* Well, I wish you'd been thinking more about the kids that night when you were looking at *porn* on your phone when you were supposed to be tending them! I wish you'd thought more about the *kids* all those years when you were thinking about having sex with women besides their mother!"

Cheryl cannot show Craig the acceptance he craves. Craig cannot draw close to Cheryl in the way she yearns for. And many of the couples who are being torn apart by pornography are just like Craig and Cheryl in this way.

A smoke detector is constantly monitoring, and yet it remains silent when the air is clean. However, once there exists in the air the problematic element that the detector has been designed to identify, the alarm is sounded. The alarm won't be quieted until the problem is addressed, the smoke is cleared, and the air is clean once again.

Within every one of us is a psychological system that is designed to maintain the connection in our most important relationships. When things are fine between us, we can function as usual. When the connection is threatened, an inner alarm is sounded. It won't be quieted until the problem is addressed, a sense of connection reestablished, and things are clear between us once again.

For most men, the inner detector is monitoring: "Am I acceptable to you? Am I the man you want me to be? Am I the good guy in your eyes? Do I measure up? Am I getting it right? Are you satisfied and content with me?" With this as priority number one, I'm never surprised when I hear men say, "If the wife ain't happy, ain't nobody happy." There's a strong element of sincerity in their joking.

However, he has now disclosed or been discovered to have a pornography problem. The inner alarm has sounded: "I messed things up. She disapproves of me. Look at what I did to her. And the scab gets ripped off again for her when I'm around her and she talks about it to me. I'm the source of her pain. I don't want to bring her down any more than I have already. Her sadness is bringing me down. It's as though we've become enemies over this issue.

"Well, what can be done now to address the problem? Can the air ever be cleared of this smoke? Can the connection be reestablished? Is there anything that can be done to help things be good between us again? This is the person who matters most to me in the entire world. I have to try: I'll give her time and space to calm down. I will stay away in hopes that things will cool off. As terrible as this seems to her now, maybe it can blend into the background as time goes on. She'll see other things about me again and remember that I'm not so bad. If we can just focus on other things, the positive aspects of life we share and can continue building together . . ."

All the while, there is an inner detector in most women. Here's what it's monitoring: "Are we close? Is he there for me? Will he listen to my concerns? Do we share? Do we talk? Are we together? Working as one? Do I know what's going on with him?"

Unfortunately, when he gives her time and space—the very method by which he is hoping to reestablish the good connection they once had—the inner alarm sounds for her: "He won't let me in! He doesn't care about what I'm going through! He downplays my feelings. I'm disconnected from him! He doesn't want to talk! He won't take my input! He shuts down when I approach him! He's pulling away. He is more distant than ever!"

From this perspective (the only perspective, by the way, that she's capable of at this point), what can be done to address the problem? She can feel the person who is most important to her slipping away. She has to do something: "I'll keep talking, reaching for and calling out to him. Bringing up my concerns. I'll express to him how much I'm hurting. I'll amplify my calls of distress. I'll do anything I can to get through to him in hopes that he'll hear me and respond by coming toward me so that we can be close again . . ."

In and of itself, her behavior is not a problem. Texting him to see if he's at risk of having a problem today or asking if he is attracted to a woman who just walked by are simply reflexive behaviors fueled by a very important instinct: to protect their connection and preserve their relationship. She's trying to bring him closer in the best way she knows how in that distressing moment. Her attempts to rebuild the broken connection originate from a reflexive drive to resecure her bond to her husband, the most important person in her life. The only problem is that her actions trigger a different reaction in him.

Likewise, in and of itself, his reflexive behavior is not the problem. By not bringing up the issue and focusing on other things, he's trying to reassure her and minimize the damage. But his reaction triggers an even stronger reaction in her than the one that provoked her initial reaching out in the first place!

Here are two people with legitimate needs and sound relationship instincts. The problem is that their reflexive behavior doesn't clear the air. It actually creates more smoke, leading each of them to pursue more vigorously the tactic for connecting that is unintentionally further impeding the connection. They are two well-meaning people who are doing their very best. Over time they may come to see each other as enemies in this process, but it is really only the cycle between them that is the enemy.

WE MAY "GET IT," YET STILL NOT BE ABLE TO GET OVER IT

Based on what I've described so far, it may seem that we could move a long way toward helping couples interrupt their negative cycle by simply explaining to them the difference in what they are seeking from each other, the gap between them regarding what each needs most from the relationship. He could draw closer to her and make sure she feels like they're together as a couple through the thick and thin of this problem. She could approach him and tell him her needs in a calm, nonthreatening way.

Sounds simple enough. However, while such explanations and understanding may help, they are rarely enough to keep couples from escalating into negative cycles. To understand why, it's important to explore the way our relationship instincts work.

Our relationship instincts are inborn, and we can see them in operation from a very young age. What happens when a child is thrust into a new and unfamiliar situation? Suddenly, relationship dependency needs take precedence over everything else. Children look instinctively to that one person, the single most important person in their lives, the one with whom they have bonded, who provides the solid external basis for the emotional security they feel internally. If they check in with mom or dad or another primary caregiver and get reassurance, it's almost as though they've now taken a deep breath of relationship oxygen. They are freed up from that most basic, primary need and they can now explore the room, socialize with the strangers there, and enjoy themselves. They're now free to be themselves: relaxed, happy, creative, and resourceful.

If a child is not able to reconnect with his mom and get the reassurance he needs from her, his distress will increase and his "attachment behavior" will escalate. His cry amplifies. If she's out of sight, his searching intensifies. The rest of his world closes down and he adopts a very narrow focus. If he was eating, now he's "all done." If he was playing, he's no longer interested. He'd rather be alone and lick his emotional wounds than socialize. Quite literally, at this point, nothing else matters to him.

Human infants need relationship oxygen as frequently as polar bears need to breathe. Polar bears can certainly submerge and swim beneath the surface of the water, but only for about two minutes before they have to come back up to breathe. Babies can't go long without reconnecting to Mom or we'll see (and hear!) evidence of their distress. Older children are becoming more independent. They're more like seals, who can stay underwater for half an hour. Older children can go a little longer, but they still come back for relationship oxygen regularly. If they don't get it when they need it, what happens? If Mom is busy, they'll tug on her leg and whine to get her attention.

As adults, we're no longer like polar bears or seals, but neither do we transform into jellyfish or some other completely air-independent sea creatures. We are more like whales, who can stay submerged for a couple of hours. We may seem more self-sufficient and less needy because we can operate longer between those deep breaths of relationship oxygen. However, we need them just as intensely, especially when we're in distress.

In the 1960s, John Bowlby, the pioneering attachment theorist, suggested that our relationship needs and our dependence on key figures in our lives continues "from cradle to grave." Researchers since that time have continued to amass evidence verifying Bowlby's claim. It's universal: Throughout our entire lives we have a healthy need to feel that we are safe and secure in our primary relationships. If we're not experiencing a desperate sense of neediness, it's probably because we sense that our primary attachment is secure!

We point this all out to demonstrate why it's so hard for husbands and wives to set their own perspectives aside, empathize with their spouses, and make sure their partners get what they need. When it feels like giving that very thing would deny each what's most important to them, the relationship oxygen they've been feeling deprived of and are now gasping for . . . forget it!

They can't do it. Being understanding and accommodating of their spouses' needs becomes mission impossible at that point.

And so we see loving, intelligent, creative, well-intentioned husbands and wives locked in a to-the-death struggle (to the death of the relationship, at least) because each feels so threatened by the way the other approaches the issues surrounding the pornography habit. Unless these negative cycles are interrupted, neither spouse can hope to get what they need from the relationship. They will remain deprived of the peace, closeness, and healing that they both so urgently need.

How Not to Break a Negative Cycle

These negative cycles don't have to continue. However, some of the common-sense ways in which we try to interrupt the cycle don't work very well. For instance, trying to explain to a spouse why she has nothing to fear when she's afraid doesn't really work. Neither does telling her that her concerns are silly or unrealistic, or in other ways trying to talk her out of her reaction. Amplifying our communication (our voice, our language, our emotion) in an attempt to get through to our spouses is generally counterproductive. We think, understandably, that if we can just get our point across, our spouses will finally "get it." Suddenly they will feel loved, secure, and at ease because we hit that sweet spot we've been aiming at. So we keep shooting *our* arrows to try to hit *their* sweet spots. These are the exact messages that would reassure *us,* after all.

On the other hand, we may try to "suck it up" and "bite our tongue" and simply be the more understanding, patient one—the bigger man (or woman) in the relationship. "I'll give more, and I'll take more of what hurts without lashing back, and thus we won't be fighting and the relationship can heal." That may be a worthy effort, and it's certainly admirable, but it usually can't be sustained.

It can't be sustained because the reasons we get into intense conflicts—or at least have the urge to fight even when we don't—are *very* important. The intensity of our emotional reaction to a relationship provocation is usually proportional to how important the relationship is to us and how threatening that event is to the relationship. Intense emotions rise when we start to lose hope of getting the relationship oxygen we need from our marriage. This is why it doesn't work to just try to restrain our natural reactions at such moments. It's also why using logic to rationally explain our responses to our partner doesn't work either. This is not a matter of decision making. It's rooted deep in a reflexive emotional survival response that supersedes anything rational or logical. Pretending that we're not whales, that we're jellyfish and can stay submerged even longer when we're in need of air, doesn't make us jellyfish.

Furthermore, it doesn't give our spouses the opportunity to build the bond between us by responding to our need and meeting it. It denies them the chance to touch the depths-of-our-soul sweet spot when it's really in need of being touched. To pretend we don't have needs doesn't make our needs go away, nor does it help us get those needs met. It just leaves our craving lingering, getting stronger, building toward a future gasp for relationship oxygen that may be even more uncontrollable, uncontrolled, and potentially destructive.

HE CAN GIVE HER RESCUE BREATHS

In coming chapters we will explore in great detail how to recognize what's fueling your negative cycles as a couple and how to interrupt them. For now, we'll simply coach the offending partner about how to take some first steps toward healing and a return to closeness.

One of the most challenging dynamics couples face in the early months following the discovery of a pornography problem is the emotional trauma inflicted on their relationship. The wife isn't only dealing with her reaction to the pornography. She is also deeply affected by the secrecy, hiding, and lying that accompanied the pornography use. This realization can transform an otherwise stable and confident woman into someone who questions her sanity.

Let's revisit the metaphor of the polar bear, seal, and whale to better understand the impact of secrecy and betrayal on a committed relationship. As you remember, children require regular reassurance of the connection and presence of their primary attachment figure. This is essential in their process of building a secure attachment and experiencing healthy relationships with others. Because they are in the forming stages, they require more "relationship oxygen," much like the polar bear requires more breaths of actual oxygen to survive.

Of course, as children move through adolescence and into adulthood, they require less "relationship oxygen," especially if the people they love continue to be available to them and care how they feel. Adults in healthy relationships know they can leave and always return to the relationship, trusting that it will be in the same place they left it. Like a whale, even though they still need regular breaths of this "relationship oxygen," they have more flexibility and endurance than a polar bear or seal. This is truly the joy of a secure, committed relationship: to know that the one you love is fully available to you and only you.

After a pornography problem is either disclosed or discovered in a committed relationship, the wife has the emotional breath knocked out of her and goes from the relationship oxygen capacity of a whale to that of a polar bear. In other words, due to the traumatic nature of the betrayal, she cannot see the relationship she once thought she had. As a result, she requires regular reassurance that she's going to survive and have some kind of relationship air to breathe.

In reaction to losing her emotional breath in the wake of this discovery, a wife will commonly begin seeking reassurance that she is going to be okay in her relationship. Some of the most common ways a betrayed partner seeks out relationship reassurance and emotional safety include:

- Checking computer histories to see if there is still an ongoing threat of betrayal.
- In-depth questioning to know what he's done and whether he's still involved in the problematic behaviors.
- Checking cell phone records to investigate any suspicious activity.
- Obsessing about her body and appearance as a way to "compete" with the threatening images so she doesn't lose her connection to her partner.
- Withdrawing from him to protect herself from further rejection.
- Attacking him in anger to let him know how much he has hurt her.

These reactions are simply her reflexive way of gasping for relationship oxygen to help her breathe and have the stability she once enjoyed. The discovery of lies and secrecy has completely changed how she sees her relationship. Before knowing about the secretive behaviors, she believed she had a full view of the entire relationship. She was sure she was the only one with whom he was expressing his sexual and emotional desires. Her question of "are you there for me?" is now more difficult for him to answer because the relationship contract of exclusivity has been broken.

One of the reasons many men struggling with pornography problems avoid talking to their partners about their behavior is because they instinctively know that their supply of relationship oxygen is also going to be severely diminished. They don't want to lose their connection either. Every couple going through the initial stages of discovery and disclosure experiences the threat of losing the connection to each other, which is punishing for both individuals.

This is why it's critical for both individuals to seek support from others in the early stages of disclosure and discovery so they can have some "relationship rescue breaths." Although these aren't the deeply satisfying breaths of a securely committed relationship, they help stabilize the person emotionally, allow him or her to keep breathing, and provide strength to move forward. This support can come in the form of seeking a qualified counselor trained in treating pornography and sexual compulsivity, receiving group support, reaching out to clergy, speaking to friends and family who are healthy and stable, and seeking a spiritual relationship with God.

The betrayed partner is going to require more rescue breathing than the offending partner. This is because she is dealing with the sudden shift in reality. He has known of his own secret life, so even though she may react negatively and create more relationship distress for him, he isn't dealing with the complete reversal of his reality. This dramatic change in reality is so traumatizing that it often takes partners years to regain the trust and confidence they experienced before the disclosure.

The good news is that he can begin providing her with rescue breaths the moment she gets the emotional breath knocked out of her (and any other time she becomes insecure or frightened about the future). Most of the time a man will have a sense that his wife will be completely overwhelmed when he tells her about his secret life, and so he often treats the disclosure like he's throwing a grenade. He pulls the pin, tosses the grenade, hears the explosion, and then stays far away from the scene. He doesn't realize that even though he was the one who created the damage, he can also do a lot to heal it.

He needs to remember that he's a source of both comfort and pain for her. As a matter of fact, he was first a source of comfort before he became a source of pain. If he interacts with her based on the belief that he's only a source of pain, he'll keep his distance out of the fear that he will only create more pain. Most guys play down their ability to do anything for their wives, believing that they will only make things worse. This just isn't true. A husband can learn that when he respects the fact that he's a source of pain, but also activates his unique role as a source of comfort, the healing process begins for the couple.

A man may wonder what he can do to become a source of comfort when he has clearly caused so much pain. One way to understand this is to notice what would happen if he *didn't* do certain things. For example, if he didn't tell her where he was going when he left the house in the evening, things would certainly be worse for their relationship. So, here's a sampling of things a man can begin doing to provide these critical relationship rescue breaths early in the process of recovery:

- Be fully honest with her about past sexual behavior.
- Provide full accountability of his whereabouts.
- Commit to complete transparency with passwords and electronic devices.
- Show a willingness to get help by seeking professional help, clergy support, and support from family and friends.
- Demonstrate increased spiritual leadership in the home.
- Offer to do more housework.

- Plan and initiate family activities (she may feel more safe with him when the whole family is together).
- Offer to spend time with her talking about her day (if she refuses, he can leave the invitation open and offer to talk at a later time).
- Recognize that his physical presence in her life does matter. He can take a walk with her, stay in the room with her even if she's not paying attention to him, and look for ways to provide a secure presence.
- Offer to read a book together.
- Spend more time with the children (such as bedtime, reading, and other activities).
- Practice more politeness and kindness with her.

Ken and his wife, Teri, had been working through the emotional trauma of betrayal for the past six months. Her world had been flipped upside down when she discovered his sexual addiction. Even though she knew that he had viewed some pornography in the past, she had no idea how extensive and involved it had become. They experienced the ups and downs of early recovery and began to have a more stable relationship as they progressed in their individual and couple recovery efforts.

"Hey, Ken, I finally figured out a word to describe the past six months," read the text message he received from Teri on his cell phone one afternoon. He quickly asked her to give him the word and she replied with the following: "Gruesome." He froze and didn't know how to respond. He was immediately filled with self-loathing and disgust for his actions. He initially wanted to fire back a text message and ask her what she thought she was trying to do. Was she trying to torture him? Did she think that describing it this way would help their relationship? Needless to say, he was perplexed about her intentions.

He decided to just reply with a simple, "Wow, let's talk about this later tonight." He happened to have a counseling session later that day and brought in his phone to discuss the loaded interaction he had just experienced.

We began to talk about why he thought his wife would send such a dramatic text message. I asked him why she would share that with him instead of someone else. After some discussion, it became clear that she wanted him to understand her pain. She needed him to know how devastating and difficult this process had been for her. He realized that it was important for him to know that she was still hurting and that his ability to respond to her in a compassionate and understanding way would only help their relationship.

After seeing this as an opportunity to offer his wife some much-needed relationship oxygen, he called her and said he wanted to go on a walk with her that evening to talk about her process of discovering this word to describe her experience.

Teri began talking first on their walk. "I've just had this pit in my stomach that hasn't gone away since I discovered everything, and I haven't known how to make it go away. When I think of everything I've been through, I feel like those actresses in those cheesy B movies who have these horrified looks on their faces when they see they're about to die. Sometimes I feel like that was me when I discovered—and even currently think about—everything you've done. It just feels gruesome."

Ken listened carefully and simply reached out for her hand and gave it a gentle squeeze. Teri allowed him to hold her hand while he responded with a sincere acknowledgement of how awful that must be for her. "That's a horrible thing to have to experience as a wife. *Gruesome* is the perfect word to describe all of this." They just let the reality of the heaviness settle on them while they walked together hand in hand. Even though they didn't talk much on the walk, Teri reported later that it really helped to have him stay with her while she worked through the difficult emotions of reviewing what she had been through in the past six months.

As a husband begins providing additional relationship oxygen to his wife, he may begin to notice that he also breathes a little easier. Although this doesn't happen in all cases, most injured partners will respond to these types of efforts to provide emotional safety and connection, even though the responses may be difficult to detect early on. Regardless, the man can trust that his efforts to provide emotional safety make a difference and are part of counteracting the belief that he is only a source of pain.

CHAPTER 3

GETTING TO
TENDERNESS

Because our spouses are the most important people in our lives, there's a lot more to most recurring conflicts than meets the eye. The matters we keep revisiting (such as pornography) may be very important. But there's so much more driving the emotional intensity on both sides. Feelings are so heightened and reactions are so strong because the relationship stakes are so high. We naturally load a big proportion of our emotional eggs in the basket of our marriage relationship. A lot of who we feel we are hangs on how we feel it's going between us and the central character on the stage of our lives. What we want most deeply, we hope to get from this relationship. Conversely, what we fear most profoundly is that we might forever be deprived here, where it matters most. And so, gasping for emotional oxygen and desperate for relationship soothing, we dig in our nails and cling to our part of the familiar, unsatisfying pattern.

We can break the negative cycles we get into as spouses by becoming more aware of the strong feelings that are triggered by the topics that get heated between us. We can begin to acknowledge what we yearn for from our spouse and what we're afraid of missing out on in the relationship. We can have tender, revealing discussions with loved ones to help them understand exactly why the topic at hand becomes such a hot one for us. Such awareness and disclosure helps the spouse soften emotionally and respond more compassionately. In place of the old, mutually provocative cycles, we shift into a reciprocal pattern of gentleness, closeness, and soothing one another.

TALKING ABOUT DEEPER YEARNINGS AND FEARS

Lane was jobless, and his hunt for work wasn't going well. Throughout the previous five months, his wife, Shelly, had been the sole breadwinner. Lane had struggled with a pornography problem, so when Shelly arrived home at the end of the day and Lane was still in his sweats and looking disheveled, it was natural for her to question whether he'd been working on his job hunt at all. He kept telling her that he was staying away from porn, but she couldn't help but wonder on such days whether he had relapsed to that habit.

They were both feeling stressed-out and worried, and so all it took was the spark of a single comment from one or the other for the familiar, negative cycle between them to be set ablaze. For instance, Shelly might come home and ask, "What have you been doing all day?"

It was a reasonable question, and natural for her to ask it straightaway.

What *had* he been doing all day?

Well, on a typical day he'd been watching some TV, feeding the dog, thinking he should walk the dog, mostly puttering around, tinkering to see if he could fix their old DVD player . . . oh, yeah, and playing way too much Xbox. And throughout the day, of course, feeling guilty that he wasn't being more effective. Trying to psych himself up to make phone calls about job openings. Vowing that tomorrow he would get up earlier and exercise, then hit it hard and "put himself out there" with potential employers when he was feeling at his best, instead of risking interacting with executives who might hold his future in their hands when he was feeling like this, feeling so . . . blah about himself.

After that kind of day, Shelly gets home, looking all sharp in her business suit, and asks, "What have you been doing all day?"

What does Lane say? What *can* he say?

Frankly, he's tongue-tied. As he stammers, she continues: "You do realize we've burned through our savings and now the credit-card balance is over fifteen thousand dollars. I'm getting burned out in my work, especially when it feels like my paycheck has to cover everything. Did you look at pornography today? Did you struggle with temptation? Please tell me that at least you're doing well at avoiding that."

Now, that, he can answer. "I told you, it hasn't been a problem for two and a half—three weeks now." She walks over to the living room area and notices Xbox discs strewn across the bookshelf. She knew he wouldn't be that careless about evidence of his pornography use if he was caught up in that addiction again.

"Yeah, you say that. But how can I be sure? You didn't tell me in the first place until I discovered it for myself."

Of course, this cycle can escalate further—much further. He could defend his addiction recovery efforts and his job-hunt attempts; she could argue that she has plenty of reasons to be concerned. He could say that perhaps he should just give in to urges if she assumes that he's guilty anyway. She could say it's that flippant attitude about fidelity that makes her worry that he might be headed toward an affair. He could accuse her of blowing his problem way out of proportion. She could accuse him of being calloused, not the guy she thought she was marrying, if he doesn't get why this is a big deal to her.

In the end, of course, these arguments would get Lane and Shelly nowhere—which is exactly what happened. Neither one felt understood or supported, and the wedge between them kept deepening.

We could have started on either side to try to exit their negative pattern, but where Shelly had been so hurt by Lane's pornography use, I was hoping that Lane might take the first steps to de-escalate their cycle. In order to have any hope of doing that, I knew that we would have to get down to the tender emotions that fueled his defensiveness.

I tried to explore what Lane had been feeling but had so far had a hard time putting into words. "What's that like for you, Lane, to be at home while Shelly's out there working? To be hoping and working to get a job and to not even have a promising lead after five months—that must be very difficult for you."

Lane nodded, eyes downcast. "It's been so tough. At first I thought this was just going to be a bump in the road. I've never gone more than a couple of weeks between jobs. But I have very few connections here. All my friends are in Colorado. Maybe it's the economy, but I've also started to worry that maybe it's me. Maybe I don't have what it takes to succeed. You know, your mind starts playing tricks on you like that. Most of the friends I keep in touch with seem to be weathering the financial storms right now. What's wrong with me? By age twenty-eight, shouldn't we be in a more stable situation? Most of my friends back home own their own places by now. Here we are still paying rent, and struggling even then, only making it because Shelly's out there bustin' her behind. I start feeling like a disappointment to her. I can get pretty down on myself."

"That is really hard for you. To sit there feeling like, 'Maybe I don't have what it takes to succeed and maybe Shelly's worse off for being with me.' That hurts." The feeling was palpable in the room. Shelly looked intently at Lane. His face was red and his eyes were glistening. After a minute, I continued, "Boy, it's tough to sit there feeling that emotional pain for very long. And even tougher to get on the phone to make phone calls or look for places to send your résumé when you're feeling that way. It's a lot easier to distract yourself by playing Xbox or even get into the tug-of-war with yourself about whether to walk the dog or not. Thinking about the pull of pornography, do you think that perhaps you're even more vulnerable to it at times when you're feeling bad like that, because of the escape and the high that it would provide?"

"No question, I'm more at risk when I'm stressed-out like that," Lane acknowledged.

"What would it be like for you to share those down feelings with Shelly at the end of the day when she gets home? Everything we talked about just now: 'Shelly,'" I role-played, "'I'm here wishing I were more on the ball so that I had something better to show you at the end of the day, so that I could measure up in your eyes. But instead I feel ineffective and worried that I may continue to fail in my efforts to find work. I compare myself and find myself wanting, and I'm afraid that you will compare me and find me wanting too.' What would it be like to go to her with those raw feelings and open up to her? Have you done that before?"

"I haven't, because she's already burdened with so much. I've burdened her with so much. I've just felt like this is something that I need to deal with on my own. It's my problem, I need to work through it. But do you know what, I know what kind of woman she is, and we've been close enough before where we've been a support like that for each other. When my younger brother died, I cried on her shoulder and she was really there for me. We cried together. . . . I needed her so badly then and she was such a support.

Maybe I need her just as much now, in a different way. Maybe I need to start doing that—talking to her. I think I could try that."

Then I turned to Shelly. "What would it be like for you to hear about Lane's day? What if he opened up to you like that about his struggles and feelings?"

Shelly's response was immediate. "I wouldn't like hearing it. I really want a man who is there for me. I have never liked playing the role of the strong one in our relationship, and right now working full-time while he's out of work . . . it just heightens this imbalance even more. I want to go to him at the end of the day and have him be my soft place to land. I can barely hold my own head above water emotionally these days; I can't keep him afloat. I don't want to be the one who has to be strong for both of us anymore."

Shelly's voice sounded crisp and sharp. Her response made complete sense, but I was shocked. I hadn't seen it coming at all. I thought we had been building a bridge that Lane could use when he was feeling bad and needed support. This would be a genuine, relationship way to meet the needs that he was trying to escape by going to his distractions and addictions. I thought that if he could be sincere about the tender feelings that were going on inside for him instead of being defensive, it might interrupt their cycle. And now it was a bit of a shock to discover that Shelly was by no means ready for it. Unfortunately, we were at a time in that therapy session when I needed to be wrapping things up. I knew another client was waiting for me in the lobby. Perhaps what I had been hoping for could still happen, but it didn't look like it would be happening anytime soon. I ended by empathizing with Shelly's need for support and then summarized by saying that they both needed a lot of support right now but were also both feeling like they didn't have a lot to give. The mood was pretty low for both of them as we ended.

After the session, I wondered whether I should have cautioned Lane against opening up to Shelly about his emotions at the end of the day, at least for now. Would it be disastrous if he showed his vulnerability in that way, only to have her respond harshly because she was in such a state of need at the time as well? I suspected that it would set them both back. I worried that perhaps I'd done more harm than good because I'd gotten him to open up about some pretty tender feelings but then missed the cues that she might not be ready yet to be receptive and supportive.

Vulnerability Evokes the Nurturing Instinct

Lane and Shelly walked into my office at the beginning of the next session hand in hand. They were also smiling. This couple was full of surprises for me. "He came to me this week," she said as we talked about what had gone differently. "When things were hard, we talked about it. He didn't just escape with the TV or the Xbox—or even worse, with porn. He told me when he felt discouraged and gave me the chance to be there for him."

"What was that like for you?" I asked.

"Oh," Shelly beamed, "it felt so nice that he let me in. I just held him and told him how sorry I was that he was struggling. That I knew how hard this was for him, and how much I admired him that he hasn't given up. I also reminded him of all the hard things he's done in the past. Building his own catering business from the ground up. Rehabing after his motorcycle accident. This is no different—the pornography or the unemployment. He can conquer these challenges, I know he can. I really believe in him. I know he will."

"How was that for you?" I asked Lane.

"It would have been nice to hear from anyone, but coming from Shelly it meant the world to me. On her own she's a strong person; on my own I could do a lot of good things, I'm starting to feel that again; but together it feels like we're invincible, especially with God in our corner. We're going to make it through this down time together, I'm sure of it."

That ended up being the final session for Lane and Shelly because they couldn't afford to continue counseling. I knew that there was no guarantee that this new direction would continue, but I was really happy that they had tasted again what it is like to open up to each other, give and receive support, and work together as one.

It fascinates me that Shelly reacted so differently during the real interaction than she herself had predicted when I asked her about how she might respond. It's not always safe to open up about vulnerable feelings because sometimes our spouse is not in a place where he or she can view us compassionately and respond supportively. However, my experience with Lane and Shelly reminded me how powerful tenderness can be. While attacking or retreating tends to elicit a similarly reactive response in a partner, genuine vulnerability tends to evoke, almost involuntarily, compassion and support. When distress is expressed in its most honest form, in a tender way, it evokes in the receiver a nurturing response. Vulnerability, when we're able to truly take it in, naturally and predictably evokes from within us our nurturing instinct.

Of course, it's difficult to maintain the purity of emotional distress. It's difficult to stay emotionally naked, even in front of a spouse we've been with for years. Our minds naturally want out of distress. We go, for example, from hurt, which feels vulnerable, to anger, which feels powerful. We move from afraid, which feels vulnerable, to withdrawn and resentful, which enables us to feel protected from the view of whoever was making us anxious. We want to feel safe instead of exposed. We want to feel powerful instead of weak.

However, when we attack and demand, the self-protective instinct in our beloved will be evoked. We make it virtually impossible for them to support and nurture us. It's just natural and automatic.

Here's a metaphor I often share with clients: Imagine that you're driving along a remote stretch of road. You come upon a car pulled over, hood raised. As you approach, the driver of the car looks you straight in the eye, points the tire iron he has clenched in his fist directly at you, and then uses it to try to wave you over to the side of the road. Of course you understand his distress. You've been there yourself before. But what does his firm and demanding bid for help evoke in you? What would your natural response be? As I painted the picture, your instincts were telling you something. What was it? Tune in for a moment to your gut. What is it telling you to do as you see this guy pointing his tire iron at you and jerking it toward the side of the road?

That's right: *Keep driving. Pass right on by. In fact, accelerate!*

Okay. Now imagine a slightly different scene. You're driving along the same road; you see the same car with the hood raised. As you approach, you see the downcast face of the driver. You sense how distraught he is. Looking at his eyes, it's unmistakable. No demand whatsoever—just vulnerability. Tune in now. What are your instincts telling you to do? You may decide to keep driving, and there are lots of good reasons to do so, but to do that you'd have to override a powerful nurturing instinct that may have been evoked. You are much more likely to pull your car to the side of the road and approach this second driver—not only because you're a good, caring person, but partly because of the way his state of need was conveyed to you.

This is one of the main tragedies of addiction. If a husband turns to an addictive substance or behavior when he's struggling or in need of support, he denies his wife the opportunity to nurture him. Women, in particular, have an extremely strong nurturing instinct. If a man denies his wife the opportunity to do what she instinctively craves, he is diminishing the quality of her marital experience. It can be heart-wrenching for a woman who naturally yearns to nurture to live with a man who doesn't come to her. In fact, women who are denied regular opportunities to nurture might even get downright cranky! Many wives have agreed that they've felt an emotional distance or wall in their relationship that has distinctly affected the level of joy and vitality they've felt in their marriage. They don't even want their husbands to do as Lane wished he could: to just handle hard things on their own. No! They want to be a part of the process. Remember, closeness, togetherness, supporting each other is that relationship oxygen that most women need in order to feel secure, complete, and confident.

FEELING BETRAYED MAKES IT HARDER TO DRAW CLOSE

It's helpful for couples to work together on monitoring the level of comfort with physical and emotional closeness in the relationship. Since it's perfectly normal for recovering couples to experience a wide range of distance and closeness, it benefits both partners to notice and talk openly about what they're each experiencing in relation to the other.

Scott was working to restore trust with his wife, Kerri, after her discovery of his pornography addiction over two years ago. He had experienced a long stretch of complete abstinence from pornography, but relapsed after about a year and began secretly viewing pornography again. This relapse, which he kept hidden from his wife and therapist, lasted several months. He eventually disclosed his secret, which immediately triggered a second, more serious, marital crisis.

When they returned to therapy, Kerri was convinced there was no way to trust Scott ever again. After an initial period of him checking in regularly with her about his progress, it became clear that she wasn't going to believe anything he said. His efforts to convince her of his faithfulness seemed to have no effect on her. Despite her indifference, he continued to report his behavior to her on a regular basis.

"I don't know what else to do. I want her to know I'm being honest now and that I have no secrets," Scott reported in one of our weekly sessions. But Kerri maintained an emotional and physical barrier between her and Scott. She figured that the distance would protect her from getting hurt again.

Both seemed anxious, raw, and unsettled. This was such a different couple from the pair I remembered working with earlier when Scott was first beginning his recovery work. It was clear they both could use some soothing and security.

My efforts with them focused on shifting Scott away from trying to convince Kerri of his abstinence from pornography. I explained to them that it's impossible to prove that something *isn't* happening. Instead, I explained to him that most of his wife's distress came from losing her connection to him when he turned away to seek out pornography. To help heal the impact of that disconnection, I invited Scott to consider being more emotionally and physically accessible and responsive to her, even if she didn't want to respond back to him.

Scott immediately worked on being more open with Kerri in more areas of his life, including his feelings and thoughts. She didn't respond much to his openness and would often just listen without making eye contact. As this progressed, I eventually asked her how she felt around him when he was being more open to her. "It's awkward because I don't know what to say. But it's better than him being closed all of the time. I guess it's nice."

This change in focus was difficult for her and, if anything, seemed to make her more insecure initially as the focus drifted from having him report on whether or not he had viewed pornography that day, which was previously her only indicator of how well he was doing. Exchanging the constant checking with more emotional openness wasn't an easy transition. However, both of them began to notice some subtle differences.

They began to experience a new feeling in their relationship that didn't exist when he was looking at pornography or when he was avoiding her, hoping she would never bring it up again. This was a new opportunity for him to show her how different and accessible he could be.

And when she felt insecure about their past and wondered if he was still faithful to her, she began to bring it up to him. Instead of creating more distance between them by being defensive, he began to see that his responsiveness to her emotional alarms was the very thing that would not only soothe her but also restore some trust.

Even though it didn't work perfectly to begin with, Scott stayed with it. One time, Kerri accused him of being preoccupied with another woman they saw jogging by their home. Scott remembered that he could actually increase their closeness by reducing his defensiveness, working instead to let her know that he imagined how difficult it must be for her to have these worries. He stayed physically close to her, kept the pace of the conversation slow, and reassured her that he was still faithful to her in his thoughts and actions. He made efforts to communicate to her that he felt remorse for her pain and reassured her that he was available to talk anytime she wanted to.

As Scott worked to stay emotionally open, Kerri began to see how often she became anxious and wanted to pull away. As a matter of fact, she described it as "wanting to get in my rowboat and row to my little island by myself where no one can hurt me." She said that this was how she had survived both the initial discovery of his addiction and the subsequent betrayal of him hiding his addiction for so many months following the commencement of treatment.

When she revealed this internal metaphor, describing her experience of wanting to move away from him, he became more clear about how to respond to her when she felt afraid. He suddenly began to see the times she would start pulling away from him because she felt emotionally unsafe. He recognized that he could be a powerful source of safety for her by noticing the distance and seeking to be more available to her.

It became more common for her to tell him when she felt like "rowing out to her island." She knew when something would trigger her anxiety and she would become quiet, pull away, and start avoiding him around the house. However, as she let him know when she was wanting to be distant from him, he used the same metaphor to draw her back in for real comfort and safety. He would ask, "Would you like me to throw you a rope to pull you back to shore, or do you need some time on your island? Either way, I'm still here." This invitation became helpful to her, as she knew that he would still be present for her when she decided to move toward him again. He didn't know when she would return, but he knew that he was there for her. That helped her, in turn, to know that he cared and wanted her to feel safe.

After some fine-tuning, Kerri ultimately stopped interrogating Scott about his behaviors. He was coming to her more often to share his emotional state throughout the day, which helped her feel closer to him. When she would struggle with insecurities, he would stay close to her and let her know that he would give her as much closeness or distance as she needed. Soon, the island metaphor became a quick way for them to resolve what used to be a significant source of pain and disconnection for both of them.

FROM CONFLICT TO CONNECTION

Another man, Carl, was very hesitant to talk to his wife, Olivia, about his tender feelings because he had so often felt judged and rejected by her. Despite that, over and over again in group therapy he had heard that he had a choice between reaching out and acting out—that he needed to learn to talk to her when he was in need or he would remain more vulnerable to relapse. He had always concluded that he was going to "do it on his own," that he would work so hard that he would succeed in his recovery without involving her. That hadn't worked out very well for Carl. Now he decided that it was time to try again.

It didn't take long before Carl had his chance. Olivia was twenty minutes late to pick him up at work on a Friday night. He had ridden the bus that morning because they had a wedding reception to go to that evening. She'd been running errands with a friend with whom she co-owned a jewelry-making business. He could feel himself getting worked up, and he wanted to keep his wits about him to increase the chance that their conversation about it might go well. He sorted it out a bit: "I know that it's not just the fact that she's running late. I know that it's not her doing this to me. I know that a big part of it is what I bring to this, my expectations."

When Carl thought about *why* he was so wrapped up in Olivia's being on time, he realized: "I wish I was so important to her that she was waiting there early at my office when I'm done with work. Maybe it sounds vain, but I want to be the most important thing in her life. I want to be on her mind. When she's late, it starts to feel like I'm an afterthought. 'There's the laundry, the kids, the customers . . . and, oh yeah, gotta pick up Carl.'"

Before she arrived, Carl remembered the last time he'd been upset when she was late. Olivia had gotten upset herself that he was making a big deal out of it. "You're a big boy," she retorted, "why can't you go down to Barnes & Noble for ten minutes and entertain yourself?"

Carl was hoping that this time would go differently. Later that evening, when they were driving home from the reception, Carl said, "I'm not trying to blame you because I'm realizing that it might be tricks my own mind starts playing on me. However, I want so badly to be number one in your life. I want to come first. I want you to feel like you can't wait to be with me. I know you can't fake that, and I'm not asking you to. But especially after a hard day at work, I just crave it. It would turn the world around for me in those moments. It's not what time you arrive to pick me up that gets to me, it's if I start to worry that I'm just not very important to you. I want so badly to be important to you."

This time, Carl could tell by looking at Olivia that her usual shield wasn't coming up. "You have no idea how stressful it is to me when I'm running late," Olivia said. "You can ask Rochelle. We were stalled at the print shop and she said, 'What's up, why are you shaking?' I said, 'Carl's going to be waiting for me in an hour and a half and we still have all these other things to do! I'll never make it!' 'Hey, girl, remember,' she was laughing, 'he's your hubby, not the Gestapo!' It's funny she put it that way because I always thought you were being a Nazi about the time thing and I didn't understand it. I felt so boxed in by it. I wondered why you were being so rigid. It felt so controlling. You know how I hate feeling controlled. So sometimes I rebelled verbally, but emotionally I kept trying so hard to measure up and get there on time so that you wouldn't be upset. And then always feeling like I was failing in your eyes—I really came to resent that. But now I can see more of what's going on for you at those times. I don't want you to feel that way any more than you do! I can see now that I should have just relaxed and called you: 'Hey, we got running late at the printer. I want you to know I'm thinking about you. I wish I were there with you rather than stuck here in traffic.' I could have let you know that I wanted to be with you just as badly as you wanted me to be there on time."

Having opened up the topic of conversation, Carl and Olivia talked about her passion for her business and the fact that Carl sometimes felt pushed to the background by it. "Sometimes I worry that you have more fun with Rochelle than you do with me. I remember when we were first married and you wanted to be around me that badly. Your friends got upset with you. We were

48

so into each other that we ignored everything and everyone else. I long to know that you feel that way about me."

"Rochelle and the jewelry don't come before you. It is something I love doing, but a big part of it is that it's easy for me. There's no pressure. I get lots of feedback that I'm getting things right and people are satisfied with my efforts. You and the kids need so much from me. I love you and them, but sometimes it feels like I don't have enough for you. I get burned out. And then, when I let down my effort or get things wrong in that arena, I feel bad about myself. I don't want to fail in my most important roles. It's not all your fault; I know part of it is the pressure I put on myself. But when I can see in your eyes that you're disappointed in me, it just kills me. That's why I lash out at you when I'm afraid you're being critical. Not because I don't care about you, but because I care so much about how I'm doing in your eyes."

Carl's honesty—first with himself and then with Olivia— helped her leave her defenses down. That made it easier for her to talk about how she started to see herself when they fought; it enabled her to talk about her deeper wants and fears as well. They'd been able to get to the tenderness beneath the conflict that kept coming between them, and they both ended up feeling like they'd bridged some of that distance.

How to Deepen Conflicts into Tender Exchanges

It can seem almost impossible to lower our defenses and communicate about what's really going on, as Carl and Olivia did. It's especially hard when strong feelings are surging, our hearts are pounding, and the pull of our reactive behaviors is very potent. Thoughts that would help us react differently are hazy and distant. It's hard to keep our wits about us and do the things that could help break the cycle.

If your house were on fire and the flame were starting to creep up your pant leg, you would be glad you had long ago learned some basic, easy-to-remember steps that might save your life. Without having to make a decision or even give it much thought, you could stop, drop, and roll. Whew!

From now on, when feelings are rising (or perhaps after the fact, when you and your spouse are ready for a do-over), try to remember: heat, hurt, and hope.

The *heat* is the emotionally intense situation or interaction that could trigger you into the negative cycle. Something's heating up your feelings, and it could prompt both of you to do those familiar but unhelpful things you do. For instance, "You're answering calls from the kids every five minutes! It makes me want to give up and cut short our night together." That's the heat.

Yelling can be a response to the heat, but so can self-righteous disdain, withdrawal, and refusing to talk. You'll know you're getting heated when emotions feel strong, urgent, and reactive. You may think you're trying to avoid getting heated when you give your spouse the silent treatment. However, when we talk about the heat here, we're referring to whatever provokes in your spouse the response that you find disturbing and keeps the negative cycle going between the two of you.

The next thing to look for is the *hurt*. What are you worried that this hot situation says about your relationship? Why does the behavior hurt your feelings? "I start to feel like I'm not important to you. I get feeling like you'd rather spend your time communicating with someone else. Being with me is not engaging enough to keep your interest." When you get right down to it, the hurt is less about the behavior itself than what that behavior says about the relationship. Something in this event or interaction became an indicator to you or your spouse that something is off between you. That's the hurt.

The *hope* reminds you to convey to your partner that you still genuinely want and need from him or her whatever you sense is missing between you. It's a chance for you to reiterate how important your spouse is to you and how much the relationship means. You may have to quiet yourself and search deep for those softer longings that involve your partner. Furthermore, it will be an emotional risk to let your spouse know how much he or she means to you. But it's one of the few things that can help both of you ease out of an intensely emotional negative cycle. "It means so much to me when I know that I have your undivided attention. It makes my whole day. And that's because you are the number-one person in my life." That's the hope.

Consider the following examples of couples who are able to stand up to the impulse to react to each other in their same old ways. Instead, they're able to acknowledge that tender feelings have been piqued (the heat), talk about the relationship significance of events (the hurt), and express their desire for connection and closeness (the hope).

Carl and Amy: Because Carl worked the graveyard shift on an assembly line at a food-packaging plant, he would sleep in the afternoon and evening and then wake up at 9:00 p.m. to go to work. He always felt better when Amy was there and they could chat and touch base as he was getting ready for his day. If either of them anticipated earlier in the day that they might want to make love that evening, they would let the other one know so that Carl could set his alarm earlier than usual and Amy could be there. Most evenings Amy was there when Carl's alarm went off. It had become part of their routine when he had gotten the job six years ago and had remained so since.

Lately, however, more and more often Amy was out with friends when Carl woke up and would get home just in time to see him off at 9:30. One night, she got home just after he'd left. What made matters worse in Carl's eyes was that he had set his alarm for 8:30 after hinting to Amy at lunchtime that he was in the mood.

Because she had missed seeing him off that night, Amy hadn't realized until the next day how upset Carl was. She didn't remember even catching his earlier hint, so she felt attacked and immediately got defensive. Then Carl felt like his concerns were being trivialized, and he got more defensive. By the time they remembered that they had planned to apply the "heat, hurt, and hope" idea when talking about things like this, they'd already become pretty heated. They decided to give it a shot anyway.

Carl started: "It may seem like I'm overreacting when I get so upset that you weren't here and didn't pick up on what I thought were pretty direct hints about wanting to be with you last night. But it's only because I start to worry that you don't care to be a part of my life. You're everything to me, and it feels so reassuring to me when I know that I come first in your life, too."

Amy took a minute to think. "I got defensive because it started to seem like you wanted me there to wait on you when you're getting ready for work. I didn't neglect you on purpose; I just lost track of time when I was with my friend. I get scared when you're so irritated; it seems like it means I'm a disappointment to you. It's easier to think that you're being unreasonable than to admit to myself that I might be letting you down. After all, you're the most important person in my life, and I so want you to be happy with me and think I'm a wonderful wife.

"I get where you're coming from, too," Amy continued. "You're so bothered because you start to get scared that you're not as important to me as you want to be. I do want you to know that you are the only one who matters most to me. Even if I miss seeing you one night—and I can't promise that won't happen ever again—there is no one in the world who holds anywhere near as important a place in my life as you. That's why I get so down when you're mad at me about something I've done that bothers you."

Carl responded, "I don't think I've realized how much of an

impact my anger has on you. I guess you've kept trying to explain it to me, but now I think I'm getting it more. It's crushing to you because your heart and soul are wrapped up in how you're doing in my eyes. It seems to me like I'm just getting upset over feeling neglected, and it comes across to you as a big stamp of 'failure,' 'loser,' 'you got it wrong—again!' And I do know you're on top of the world when you get things just right in my eyes."

•　•　•

Elise and Bill: Elise called Bill one afternoon at work and asked him to get online and look at pictures posted by Bill's sister, Vivian. They showed a get-together at a restaurant. In the pictures were Vivian, Bill's other two sisters, and Bill's brother's wife—in other words, all of the women in Bill's family of that generation except Elise. Bill felt sick inside when he saw their smiling faces and arms around each other's shoulders because he knew how they had made Elise feel. He also felt incapable of making this situation better no matter how he handled it. There was silence on both ends of the line for a while. Bill sighed a couple of times. Then he could tell that Elise was crying. "Look," he finally said, "you know that they're like this—exclusionary. It says more about them than it does about you. Consider the source. Try not to let it get to you." Elise knew that Bill was in the middle of his work day, and it felt like he was just trying to wrap up the conversation and get off the phone with her, so she ended the call.

When they both got home that night, Elise said, "I know it must be hard when I bring stuff like that to you when you're at work and I'm in an emotional flare. But I can't imagine not touching base with you when I get the rug pulled out from under me like that emotionally. I desperately need to know that at least you're there for me when I'm hurting like that."

Bill nodded. "It was like a kick in the gut to me too when I looked at those pictures. I know it might seem like I was trying to downplay your feelings, telling you not to worry about it and all. But I feel like a firefighter. I just want to put out the hurt. And when I can't—when I could hear you crying—it feels so bad to me, like I'm no help at all to you, like I can't be there for you in the way you need me to be. It is a relief to get off the phone with you at those times. I'd rather make it all better, but when I know I can't do that, it's hard for me to sit there with you and witness the person who means the most to me hurting like that."

• • •

Vern and Julia: Vern's father had worked as a bookkeeper for years, so his questions to Julia about how she was running her graphic design business were thought-provoking. The discussion over Sunday dinner ended up being inspiring and productive, she thought. But on the drive home Vern was silent. As they pulled into their own driveway, he said, "It was great to see how many helpful ideas my dad had for you. The sad part to me was that I was learning about most of those things for the first time myself! I didn't know you guys had hired another artist part-time. I didn't know about your big contract for the summer festival. It might seem like I'm overreacting, but it really deflated me to feel like I'm not a part of your life like I want to be. On the one hand I was drinking in all of the information, but on the other hand my heart was aching that I have to overhear a conversation to know what's going on with the most important person in my life. I'd just love to feel like I got that window into your life more of the time."

It was an aha moment for Julia. "It's funny," she responded, "I get embarrassed telling you about the nitty-gritty stuff because it feels like I'm just bumbling my way through all this growth. I like you to see the impressive end results, and not necessarily the blood and guts along the way. It may sound strange to you, and now as I put it into words it doesn't sound like the right thing to do, but so often I just try to deal with things on my own until I'm sure of the outcome. Then, at the unveiling, I'm really watching your response. And it's all because you're my most important audience. I want so badly to know that I'm on the right track in your eyes. I can see now that I don't have to perform for you. You want to be there throughout the whole process to help me out and cheer me on. I would love that. I need it."

· · ·

Heather and Frank: Frank was reluctant to take Heather to this year's company party. Heather's mind would be going all night, and then he would hear about all of her worries later: "Is Vicki that flirtatious around the office? Cassandra has had breast enhancement surgery, right? If Yvonne's still with her boyfriend, how come she flirts with Jack that way? How would you have acted if I wasn't there? How would the women have treated you?"

Rather than each of them stewing about it separately, as usual, Frank brought it up. "I know you get upset when I try to avoid situations that will lead to big talks between us. But I just hate it when you're reminded that you've had reasons to question my faithfulness. I feel panicky when I think that you're going to go from trusting me wholeheartedly, which feels like heaven to me these days, back to questioning my intentions or doubting my fidelity."

Heather said, "I can see why you get tired of it when I keep expressing my concerns. But I just start to feel so insecure again when it seems like I have to compete for your attention or that your affections could be drawn away from me. It's so different when I feel like I'm still everything you want. That's what I long to feel sure of, and that's what gets brought into question in my heart when we go through situations like that."

To conclude, the following chart summarizes what happens when couples are stuck in negative cycles, how to interrupt those cycles by sharing the relationship significance of topics that get heated, and how much better things go when they stay honest and connected with each other. We hope it will help you stick with your efforts to interrupt a negative cycle and communicate honestly about pornography or any other struggle, and to work past the heat, beyond the hurt, clear through to the hope.

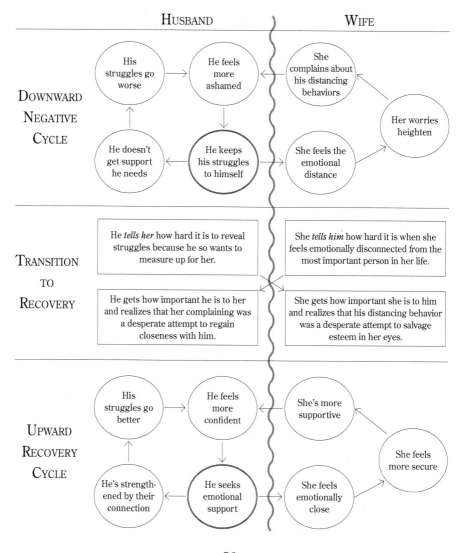

CHAPTER 4

She Needs You Now More Than Ever

It can be devastating to learn of a partner's virtual infidelity. Everyone responds differently, but there are some commonalities. Relationship trauma experts Drs. Kevin Skinner and Shondell Knowlton have noted in their research (see www.growthclimate .com) that common reactions include:

- intense feelings of fear
- feelings of helplessness
- concern about contracting a sexually transmitted disease
- an inability to look at your spouse without being reminded of his or her sexual behavior
- intrusive thoughts about your partner's inappropriate sexual behavior
- disturbing dreams about your partner's sexual behavior
- worrying that your partner thinks about other experiences and images when you are together
- tendency to be suspicious and accusing

- flashbacks in which you relive the worst parts of the experience
- being reminded of what your partner has done by stories and images in the entertainment and news media
- having a hard time being in public places with your partner because you have become highly sensitive to what he or she has done
- feeling anxious when you see sexually suggestive images
- physical symptoms such as nausea and headaches if you're exposed to things that remind you what your partner has done
- spending a lot of energy trying to avoid thoughts that remind you of your partner's behavior
- trying to act like everything in your relationship is just fine when you're around others
- engaging in behaviors that distract you from thinking about your partner's behavior (such as excessive reading, sleeping, eating, drinking)
- holding back from people who used to be close to you
- avoiding situations where you know there will be sexually suggestive images more than you used to
- avoiding sexual contact with your partner
- getting distracted easily
- having difficulty remembering who you've talked to and what you've told them
- having a hard time participating in things that you previously enjoyed
- having difficulty fulfilling important roles (such as employee or parent)
- feeling like you are different from everyone else
- feeling like you don't belong anymore when you are in social settings

- feeling ashamed and embarrassed when you are in public because of what has happened in your relationship
- using a lot of energy pretending to feel things that you think you should feel
- having difficulty falling asleep
- becoming increasingly angry in response to your partner
- being more critical in conversations with your partner
- feeling more emotionally on edge than you used to
- finding it hard to focus on what is going on around you
- feeling the need to monitor your partner's behavior
- constantly trying to read your partner's emotions

We've also seen some partners try to be more sexually aggressive, experimental, or attractive in an effort to save their relationship.

Virtual infidelity's effect on people's lives is like an octopus with far-reaching tentacles. Some effects are obvious, others surprising; some consequences are direct, while others creep up quietly, show up later, or linger mercilessly. Suffice it to say that few other things put one in such a state of profound need. When people are in that state of need, it becomes very important how their partners, the most important people in their lives, respond.

Two months ago, Steve told Lisa, his wife of four years, that he had been struggling with a pornography habit since the time he was single. Before that disclosure, Steve had thought that, despite this shameful secret, he and Lisa had a basically good marriage. Lisa had also felt like their marriage was strong. She sometimes talked about wanting to feel more connected and emotionally open with each other—wanting to feel like they were truly "one" as a couple—but she would never have guessed that Steve was struggling with something like this. He had always been spiritually devout, and his integrity was impeccable in so many other areas of life. At least it had seemed that way to Lisa.

During my first appointment with him, Steve said, "Telling her about my addiction has complicated everything." Lisa couldn't fathom why he had kept his struggle from her. She couldn't help but wonder about what he had seen and how it might have affected his view of her when they were physically intimate as a couple. She worried about what this meant for their future.

"Over the past few days, she's been really sad. She won't talk to me, won't look me in the eye," Steve said. "I've been wanting to be close to her, but when I come around it seems like it makes things worse. The other day I walked into the living room and sat down on the couch next to her when she was reading. She started to sob. Being around me just opens the wound for her again. I started to feel like she wanted me to stay out of her way. I also felt like her sadness was bringing me down. At times she's been cold, acting as though I'm not even there. I came to the conclusion that if we're going to be enemies over this, I'll stay away from her. I started to keep my distance.

"But then," Steve recalled, "last night I was at the library doing some work on a school assignment. We talked on the phone and she seemed so sad again. My instinct was to just back off and find a reason to hang up. But I was feeling spiritually in tune yesterday. Something inside me didn't let me hang up. I felt like I needed to hang in there, that there was something for me to learn. *Stick with it. Stay on the phone until you can understand a little more about what's going on with her.* So I kept waiting to see if I could elicit anything about what was going on for her and what she needed.

"She finally let me know, sobbing on the phone, that she was terribly lonely. She wanted me at home with my arms around her. Of course, I came right home. Realizing that she wanted me there with her, and the tenderness I could see in her as she expressed it, softened me. I broke down. We cried together and held each other for a long time. It felt so good to discover that she still wanted me close. Despite the hurt, she didn't want to be rid of me. It's such a relief that I don't have to banish myself from her presence as penance for what I've done. We can stay close to each other as we work through this."

WHY SHE LOOKS TO YOU WHEN SHE'S IN PAIN

If a woman has been hurt by her husband's pornography use, she feels a strong need for support from another person. Most women have a handful of people in their lives that they *could* reach out to. She could go to her mother when she finds herself feeling troubled, disheartened, or hurting. She could go to a sister or a close friend. She could seek help from a therapist. She could go to an ecclesiastical leader. Some men find it surprising, however, that their wives want most to come to them.

Of course, part of that is because her husband is the one who has been involved in pornography. It wouldn't be as fruitful to ask a friend why he started, why he kept looking, and why he didn't open up about the problem earlier. Also, it is her husband who, for his own good as well as hers, needs to know how she has been hurt by his pornography use. He needs to understand how his behavior has hurt her so that he can stay a better course in the future, make amends, and seek forgiveness from her.

However, there is another, even more important reason that she goes to him to talk about her pain. It's because he is her husband. He is her one and only. He is the one she most wants and needs to turn to when she is hurting about *anything*—even including those hurts that he may play some role in. He is, in the words of relationship researchers, her *primary attachment figure.* It is her deepest instinct to go to him. Viscerally she senses that it is a response from him alone that she wants.

This is important to remember because often a man, after hurting his wife, will feel that he has lost that privileged status in her eyes. In fact, now he may even feel like the jerk it hurts her to be around. He pulls away to spare her the pain of closeness to the perpetrator who has created her trauma. However, all of the support and consoling and listening that a myriad of other supportive people can provide won't hit the depths-of-her-soul sweet spot for her like a receptive, validating, compassionate response from him can.

CONFLICTING FEELINGS ARE BOTH LEGITIMATE

Julie walked into the office and slumped onto the couch with a big sigh. "I asked Paul to sleep on the couch this weekend because I discovered some pornographic websites on his phone. I kept my cool, for the most part, but I still want him to be far away." Another sigh. "But how far away? Kicking him out of the house doesn't seem like the right thing to do right now, for some reason. Over the months, I've tried everything. I've locked him out of the house, let him stay in our bed, had him sleep on the couch, and a couple of times I've even been more affectionate. Now I can't decide what course to take. So I guess I'm stuck."

Reactions like Julie's are not uncommon. It's no wonder she's torn: being around Paul soothes her *and* pains her; she wants him and hates him. When I suggested this, she agreed: "Yes! That's it! I want to come to him for reassurance, but I also want to punch him in the face and get him away from me. No wonder I feel like I'm going crazy!"

One of the most confusing dynamics for recovering couples is the dance of closeness and distance between them. There are moments when the injured partner seeks out her husband to talk, for touch, or simply for his familiar presence. She comes for validation of her worth and desirability. Then there are the days when she doesn't want to be in the same room with him. Disgust and dread well up within her when he comes near. She wants him to stay away. This roller coaster of emotions is jolting and confusing.

She has one foot on the accelerator of the relationship and one on the brake.

Friends and loved ones wonder why she's so heated one day, only to be cool and calm about things the next. They see her relating to him as though nothing was wrong at all, then watch her treat him like nothing will ever be the same again.

Of course, her husband is mystified as well. He gets his hopes up as she moves in close for a hug one day, and then watches those hopes crumble as she asks him to sleep on the couch the next day.

"What would happen if you let Paul be both a source of comfort and a source of pain for you?" I asked. Julie didn't quite understand how that might look. "What if, when you felt a genuine desire to be close to him, you let yourself reach out? And, when you needed a little space, you allowed yourself to ask for that space?"

She thought about this possibility for a moment. "Well, won't that confuse him?"

"What do you think you could say to him that might help him understand that you're moving toward him and away from him according to what feels right at the time? That in different moments you're going to need to get your bearings in different ways?"

After some discussion, she decided to explain it to him this way: "Paul, now that you've chosen to view other women's bodies, I am confused and insecure about whether you want to be with me. There are times I will want to come to you to talk or for a hug. And because I'm in a lot of pain, there are times when I need time and space to clear my head so I can sort out how I'm feeling and what I need to do. Your letting me move back and forth between these two needs will do a lot to help me feel more supported and may help build trust back between us."

In truth, Julie was responding to Paul as a source of comfort in both seeking closeness and also sharing her pain when she needed space. Letting Paul know that she was in pain and needed some space was actually a form of reaching out to him, to let him know she was hurting. Not only was she reaching out to him when she needed closeness, she was also reaching out to him in a different way by letting him know when she needed space. Giving her space at such times became something he could do to provide comfort for her. Paul's respectful responsiveness to her need for both closeness and space would do much to help her feel relief from the wound of betrayal as he continued to work to understand and overcome his pattern of pornography use.

WHY IT'S SO HARD TO BE THERE FOR HER

The depth of a wife's need for her husband to listen and understand makes it all the more painful when he misses the boat and fails to be there for her in that way. In the great majority of cases, it's not that he doesn't want to be there for her. He simply has his own perspective and struggles that get in the way. When the distress she feels over his pornography problem becomes apparent, he may be taken aback by the severity and depth of pain she suffers. Emotional distress is not the most comfortable river for him to swim in to begin with, and now when it looks to him like she's gasping for air and being ripped at by piranha, it's a lot for him to witness. And then to be asked to join her in the midst of that distress . . . whoa! It's enough to take his breath away.

Eminent marriage researcher John Gottman used physiological measures to assess men's and women's bodily responses to emotional conversations. He found that when the topic content was upsetting, although men might have appeared to be "keeping their cool," their bodies were taking quite a ride. Their heart rates elevated, their breathing deregulated, their blood pressure rose, they sweated. The wives of these research participants often seemed more heated and passionate, but it was actually the men who were reacting internally and physically to a much greater degree. Furthermore, the stress hormones that get dumped into men's systems when they're feeling "stressed by distress" don't dissipate as readily or quickly. The men remained amped-up over a longer period of time than their wives did (Gottman and Levenson 1988).

It may not be accurate to say that emotional upset is always more upsetting to men than it is to women, but it might be true that men are usually not as adept at handling and managing it. This all may play some role in why women and men respond so differently to emotional distress. As we discussed earlier, women instinctively share their distress to soothe it, while men instinctively try to better a distressing situation if they can, and avoid it altogether if they can't.

We're not trying to give a man an excuse to not be there for his wife when she's hurting. We're just explaining the phenomenon, in hopes that both of them can see why it's so difficult. Of course, the hope is that he'll keep trying to stay close to her so that he can get better at it than he has been. The hope also is that if she understands how challenging it is for him, she can be patient with him as he works to improve. Otherwise a wife may wonder, "How hard can it be for him to just sit there, to simply be with me as I talk about how I feel?"

It might be easier for her to be more patient when she understands that he's doing more than sitting and listening—he's trying to manage the arousal of his own nervous system. He's resisting the instinct, crying out within him, to simply apologize and promise to do better so that the discussion can be over with. He's resisting the urge to change the subject, or to tell her his problem isn't as bad as she has come to believe it is. He's resisting the urge to feel hopeless and give up the possibility of things ever getting any better. When he faces her distress up close, his inner demons drag him into a funhouse with all kinds of contorted mirrors. Reality takes new shapes that can be hard to handle.

It's quite a challenge for a man to learn to really listen to his wife's experience and how she feels about it. In the process, it is not primarily *her* distress that he is learning to tolerate, but his own. It hurts him to see her hurting. Add to that his knowledge that she is hurting over what he has done. This is the bride he treasured, the woman he most likely still treasures, although he let her down in weak moments. This is the woman he has worked to support and care for. This is the woman he has sworn—and wants with all of his heart—to protect. For the vast majority of men, this remains true despite what they may have done in the throes of craving and addiction. It was only when they were not in their right minds that they did the hurtful things they've done. And now, to witness the charred and smoldering emotional and relationship landscape in an area that was once verdant . . . that, for some men, feels like too much.

The Depth of Pain Can Overwhelm Both Spouses

Discovering Kyle's pornography problem has left Vivian questioning the very foundation of what she thought they had together. "It's changed something at a very deep level, and I don't know if we're ever going to be able to get that back," she said.

When Kyle's secret habit came out, it rocked Vivian's world. It left her doubting the man she used to trust implicitly. It made her disgusted by how sexualized U.S. culture has become. She almost smashed their TV set. She cancelled their satellite service. She actually did set his laptop behind the tire of her SUV and then drove back and forth over it several times. Then she chucked his iPhone in a lake.

Perhaps worst of all, Kyle's vulnerability to pornography left Vivian feeling insecure about herself. Every aspect of her body that she'd ever found fault with came rushing back to her mind. For a brief period, whenever she became self-conscious, she felt like an amalgamation of all of those less-than-ideal bodily features, and nothing else. All cellulite, moles, hunched posture, and wrinkles. She felt claustrophobic in her own body. Then she cursed herself for ever taking emotional risks during lovemaking. "I was playful and uninhibited. I tried to dress all sexy. What an idiot I was! I thought that only he and I shared our own little world of sexuality together. If I'd known all the fantasies that inhabited that world for him, I would never have felt free enough to be that way with him." She also questioned Kyle: "Why wasn't I enough for you?" she asked him over and over again. "What was it about these women that was so appealing that it drew you away from me and ruined what we had?"

Every time Vivian asked such questions, it wrenched Kyle's heart. "That's not what it meant to me!" he insisted. "I don't want to be with any of those women. I was just caught up in the pull of it. I told you before, I would get tunnel vision and I didn't think about you, our family, my religious beliefs. I'd get lost in it. I'm not saying that makes it right, just that I wasn't choosing it over you. I was caught up in the compulsion."

In a way, Vivian was glad that Kyle was trying to reassure her. As bad as it was during the bad times, quite often she would come back to herself and her usual view of Kyle, her usual way of feeling about herself. It was almost like they could pick right up with their old lives and move on. Miraculously to her, she found that she could even lose herself in physical intimacy with Kyle again when he was attentive and she knew he was mentally "with her." Nonetheless, the emotional rug would sometimes get pulled out from under her again by some event or some memory, and rarely did his explanations help during those down times. Quite often, in fact, his insistences made her feel worse. "You have no idea what it's like for me, do you? In a way it bugs me that you're try-ing to talk your way out of something you behaved your way into, something that has hurt me so badly. I'm not wrong for feeling this upset, and all of your talking starts to sound like rationaliza-tions and justifications—as though it's really not that big of a deal, what you've done. As though I should be able to understand that it wasn't that serious in your mind, and thus not be so affected by it. When I sense that that's where the conversation's going, it hurts even worse. I feel even more alone and wounded. Not only have you injured me, but you won't stay with me while I recover from how it's affected me. You want to put a Band-Aid on my compound fracture and pretend it's a scratch. I'm not going to let you do that, and it really offends me that you would want to."

Kyle was not trying to minimize her pain, but he started to realize that the way he was handling it was unintentionally perpetuating—and perhaps even exacerbating—Vivian's suffering. However, he didn't yet understand how to make it better. In fact, he had begun wondering whether he could.

SHE HAS TO KNOW THAT YOU GET HOW MUCH SHE'S HURTING

When I talk to couples who are working through a pornogra-phy problem in a way that enables them to feel closer than ever before, I'm always curious about what made the difference. Some cite that it is key moments of connection and sharing, with all the walls down, that are enabling them to draw together like never before and lifting their recovery to a new level.

Brian said, "It was that night in our bedroom that turned things around. For the first time, when Leslie expressed her concerns and fears, I just listened. She was sitting on the bed, so I knelt down in front of her so that we were looking eye to eye.

"I could see that she was feeling troubled about things again," he continued. "Before, I would always try to apologize, make promises and plans, and show her how angry I was at myself for what I'd done. This time I just knelt there in front of her and listened. As she described her hurts, she cried, and when she did, I cried with her. We just stayed there and cried together about the pain and hurt that my sins and secrecy had caused her."

Leslie called out in distress. Brian heard and let her know that he knew how badly she was hurting. Leslie felt soothed and a little more secure than she had before. This is a sequence that can occur over and over again. It's a virtuous circle that deescalates Leslie's distress and the tension between them, replacing the vicious circle that used to get going between them.

We truly can help heal other people's pain simply by trying to understand what they're feeling and willingly joining them where they are, in that emotion, rather than trying to make it go away.

One day I was pushing my four-year-old daughter, Sarah, on the backyard swing set. Her two-year-old brother, Sam, waddled up and planted himself on the swing next to her. Pretty soon they were both giggling and going strong. I got distracted for a minute watching the older kids play ball at the other end of the yard. I turned back in time to see Sarah dismount and walk toward the ladder to the slide. Then I realized she was in tears.

"What's the matter, honey?"

"You didn't push me!" she sobbed.

I realized then that I must have stopped switching back and forth between them during the time I'd been distracted.

"Honey, I'll push you some more. Come get back on."

"You didn't push me!!" she wailed.

"Honey, I was pushing both of you. I can push both of you."

"You didn't push me!!!" She swiped the back of her hand across a wet face.

"Honey, Sam needs a turn too. You don't want Sam to feel . . ."

Then I stopped. I realized that this was something I talk about with clients all the time. Here it was, right in front of my face: emotional distress. How was I handling it? My knee-jerk reaction had taken me straight to the default modes of explaining, defending, suggesting, and trying to make it better. Perhaps I didn't have to do any of that, I realized. Maybe she just needed to be heard, to know that what she was feeling registered with me. I walked over to the slide, put my hand on her arm, and looked her square in the eyes. "You were so sad when I pushed Sam instead of you."

"Ye-ah!" she wailed.

"You wanted me to keep pushing you."

"Uh-huh." Her sobs were winding down already.

"And you felt bad when I didn't."

"That made me sad," she said, in an almost calm voice. She sat there for a few seconds more. One more wipe of her face, and then her eyes widened as she said, "Hey, Dad, wanna watch me go down the slide?"

SITTING TOGETHER WITH THE PAIN HELPS SOOTHE IT

Some men have benefited from having a metaphor in mind, a mental handle to hold onto, enabling them to stay put when they want to run away and to listen when they want to change the subject or plug their ears. One such metaphor is the idea that listening to her pain is like clearing the gunk from the mouth of a spring. Imagine a spring of water with a great big stopper plugging it. You unclog it, only to discover that the water that flows from it is murky and yucky. You think, "This is no good; I don't want this kind of water," and decide to plug the hole back up. Here's the problem: You can't tell this by what you see from the surface, but that gunky, polluted water only goes from the mouth of the spring down about twenty feet into the ground. Beneath that, the water is pure and clean. By plugging the spring back up, not only have you left the muck still right at the surface, you're holding back the refreshing, life-giving water that could flow from deeper down. You're keeping that good water from coming out and washing away the polluted stuff. So when you sense a fresh flow of gunk, don't try to stop it. Neither of you wants it to build up. Keep the gunk coming!

Women whose husbands have hidden a pornography habit from them and lied to them about it usually have a lot of pain and anger to work through. Even when their marriage has been good in many other ways and they have a lot of positive facets to their relationship, giving them good reason to stay together and work on the marriage, it's no small thing to try to come to terms with virtual infidelity. Watching these upset feelings come out can be very distressing for husbands. If a man responds to his own distress by stepping back from the situation and giving his wife space and time to heal, it can leave her feeling worse instead of better. It's like plugging up a spring when it's trying to clear out the crap that's ready to be purged. When we fail as couples to spend lots of time together talking, processing, and sorting through feelings and questions, the wife is left with all of the gunk right there at the surface ready to burst out. And that's usually just what it does.

It had been eight years since Vanessa had caught Ray in the act of having sex with a prostitute. Then, over the subsequent three weeks he had disclosed to her other details of his sexual addiction. Now, years later, she had grown apart from the friends who had known her back then. They couldn't understand why she hadn't left Ray. Vanessa had stayed to work on the marriage partly for the sake of her kids but also because there was so much good in the life she and Ray had built together, despite his infidelity.

In the years since that time, they had been working to rebuild their marriage and become closer. Vanessa felt like the healing wasn't finished, but that they were still headed in a good direction. "Don't get me wrong," she said, "there are still things that dredge back up the hurt. I'll see something on a TV talk show about infidelity. Or someone makes a joke of it—which really stings because I think, 'They have no idea how devastating it is if they can trivialize it like that.' Or even things that may not seem related, like my teenage son smoking cigarettes and then hiding it and lying about it. It reawakens that feeling of being deceived by someone I love. When I have a hard time like that, Ray will come and rub my feet. Sometimes he doesn't say anything. Other times he'll say, 'I'm sorry you're going through this. It must be hard.' It's so great to feel that he's got my back. If I have a bad day, I can talk to him and it won't turn into a fight. He won't pretend that what happened didn't happen. It allows me to feel like, even though it's still hard, I'm not a freak for not being able to let this go and be over it. It's okay that sometimes I still hurt from it. As much as he wants me to be okay, he wants even more to know how I'm really doing. That means a lot to me. Knowing that, I can relax and not feel tense. I can feel at peace. I'm still troubled by those wounds at times, but I don't have to have the added pain of beating myself up over my current reaction. I talk to him, and he doesn't act like it's bugging him that I bring it up. That turns the world around for me. He puts me first and really listens to what I say. And he keeps rubbing my feet. I've told him, 'As long as you keep rubbing my feet, I'm not going anywhere.' It helps me feel loved and secure. It lets me fall asleep. Having my feet rubbed is like a drug."

Like a drug? Actually, it's the other way around. Drugs that calm the nervous system only do so because they mimic the soothing effect of chemicals that operate naturally within our bodies and brains when we're touched or caressed by someone we love. The pituitary gland secretes the chemical oxytocin, the "cuddle chemical" we referred to earlier in the book. When we hold hands or snuggle, doses of this relationship bonding agent are released into the bloodstream, helping us feel more connected and contented.

Just as touch can stimulate oxytocin production and release, being deprived of touch leads to depleted oxytocin levels and leaves us feeling ill at ease. In studies using rats, oxytocin relieved the rats' cravings for drugs and even sweets. Doses of the hormone consistently led the rats to opt for less of these mood-altering substances even when they were given unlimited access. Again, it's not that touch is like a drug, it's that drugs and other addictive substances mimic—and thus perhaps we use them to try to replace—the salutary effects of connecting physically with a loved one. I'm convinced that this process was a part of how Ray was helping Vanessa heal when he rubbed her feet.

Since so many men have a hard time staying close to their wives when they're in distress, I asked Ray how he had been able to stay and keep rubbing Vanessa's feet and listening. "I could see from the beginning that she was stuck in pain from what I'd done," he explained. "After she first became aware that I was cheating on her and addicted to sex, when I heard her talk about it, it was almost like watching her sit in a scalding hot tub. By bringing up the topic, she was inviting me to soak in there with her. I'd dip my toe in by listening briefly, and then I wanted to get out and get away. *Can't we focus on other things?* I thought. But then once, as I was about to walk out of the room when she was collapsed there, overcome with sadness, I realized that I couldn't in good conscience walk away. I knew that she was there because of me, and I felt the obligation to stay there with her, to sit and soak with her in the scalding hot tub if necessary. I've tried to do that ever since."

Marriage and family therapist Dorothy Becvar once described this process of sitting with someone in their distress as a "ministry of presence." It's common to assume that your presence and stillness may not be doing much good. However, physical proximity and emotional attentiveness are a soothing balm to an overworked nervous system.

Priest and author Henri Nouwen put it this way: "Being with a [partner] in great pain is not easy. It makes us uncomfortable. We do not know what to do or what to say, and we worry about how to respond to what we hear. Our temptation is to say things that come more out of our own fear than out of our care for the person in pain. Sometimes we say things like 'Well, you're doing a lot better than yesterday,' or 'You will soon be your old self again,' or 'I'm sure you will get over this.' But often we know that what we're saying is not true, and our [partner] know[s] it too. We do not have to play games with each other. We can simply say: 'I am [your partner], I am happy to be with you.' We can say that in words or with touch or with loving silence. Sometimes it is good to say: 'You don't have to talk. I am here with you, thinking of you, praying for you, loving you'" (Nouwen 2006, 15).

As challenging as it is for a man to listen and acknowledge his wife's pain, there is nothing like practice to strengthen his ability to tolerate distress. Although it might be difficult, that means time in the saddle: time spent hearing about her hurts, her worries, her insecurities that have resulted from his behavior. It also helps some men to remind themselves to simply breathe: "Take in a breath just like I'm taking in her experience. Take in oxygen just like I'm taking in what she's feeling." When we find ourselves immersed in distress, our instinct is to brace against it and hold our breath. But then we're more likely to be looking for an escape. We act like we need to get out of this situation like we need our next breath, because, in a way, we do. We get defensive, impatient, and less able to really be with our spouse. So it may be as simple as this: sit, look her in the eyes as she talks, listen, and breathe. Remind yourself to keep breathing, and hopefully that will help you keep listening.

It's also helpful to remember why a woman is so hurt by this kind of behavior: it drew *her husband* away from her. It came between her and the one person who means the most in her life. When a man can put aside his shame long enough, he realizes that her pain is not primarily about his failing to measure up in this important area of life. It's not about him being unworthy or unlovable because of his misbehavior. She's hurt and angry because she's genuinely scared. She's experiencing a clear and imminent danger of losing the connection she has with her husband, the connection that means more to her than anything else. No wonder she gets distraught and overwhelmed and agitated. Who wouldn't? After all, he means *that much* to her.

STILL WATERS, THEN FRESH WAVES OF PAIN

Bad times often come right on the heels of good. They hurt even more because the sweet aftertaste of closeness hasn't even faded. The trauma of betrayal can shift reality so quickly that injured partners may find themselves checking and double-checking again after feeling safe. Warmth and tenderness give way to a cool distance. Actually, most partners begin have *more* moments of insecurity as the relationship progresses toward a restoration of trust. Insecurity isn't a commentary on how poorly the process is going. It may just be a signal that the injured partner needs a reminder that what is happening is indeed real. When a wife expresses anew fear and pain after things have been going well, it may be that she's saying, in essence, "I was feeling safe enough with you before, given the amount of emotional armor in which I'd encased my heart. But now I've let you back into my heart a little bit more again. I've removed another piece of armor. And I'm feeling very vulnerable. The hurt and fear all comes back and seems fresh. Since I'm taking more risk than I did yesterday, yesterday's reassurances are not enough. I need your understanding and help again right now!" Responding with swift and genuine empathy during these moments provides comfort and security for the injured partner. It also reminds her spouse of the power he holds to help her heal.

When the communication of a partner's pain seems unrelenting and even seems to amplify over time, some men fear that their wives may relish being in the hurt role, or may be using their pain over the pornography habit as a club to beat their husbands with. Most of the time, that's just not true. Usually, repetition and amplification only happen when the wound gets reopened in some way or if there's a sense on the wife's part that initial communications haven't been fully received.

Grief over loss comes in waves. It recedes for a time, and life goes back to normal in many ways. But then, in time, another wave hits. When it does, it's not that the people involved will "never get over" their pain. It's not that they're harboring resentments. They're just dealing with a fresh wave of grief over the loss or worry about the future. The thing a wife will need from her husband the next time she experiences a wave of anger or sorrow is just what she needed after the first wave hit: a willingness to listen to what she's going through and feel some of it side by side—or perhaps face to face—with her.

It can be disheartening to some men—and their wives, too, for that matter—when gunk comes out of the emotional well again after they thought they'd cleared it all out. However, over time they learn that they can trust the same process every time yucky stuff comes to the surface again. Although the initial clearing can be quite an ordeal and may take weeks or even months, many of the later ones require just a brief acknowledgment and validation of the pain, and then the couple can more readily move on to other aspects of life.

Here's another way to view this process of revisiting painful memories as part of the healing process. Imagine walking up a spiral staircase. Even though you are viewing the same scene with each pass around the staircase, your perspective slowly begins to change as you move upward. Eventually, the way you view the same scene looks different from how it seemed at the beginning of the journey. Likewise, when people who have been traumatized have a chance to process the details and feelings associated with the painful events, they begin to experience a new perspective and move through the stages of healing. There is no need to set an expiration date on how much they need to talk about their pain. If they can process their pain in the presence of loving and patient support, they will move upward and gain a new perspective of themselves and the painful experience.

Research on the emotional reassurance we receive from our primary relationship suggests that security is not something we develop and then retain forevermore, like a cement foundation that a building can always rest upon. Rather, security is more like a battery that needs recharging. Security is not necessarily a place we arrive at and forever reside there. We naturally cycle back to a place of feeling insecure and needing reassurance. And we can't focus on other things until we get it. Once we do, we can get on with our lives . . . at least for a time. Until we need comfort again, that is. Eventually, most couples stop viewing the offended partner's need for reassurance as a negative thing. It's just a chance for more closeness and bonding.

One man, Jeff, expressed frustration initially that his wife, Patricia, seemed to keep falling back to not believing him when he promised her that he was making the changes he needed to in his life to leave pornography behind for good. I encouraged him to look at her ups and downs as indicators of what she needed, not what she believed. I knew from an earlier discussion with him that as a child Jeff had often been comforted by his father when he was sick to his stomach. His dad would come over and press on his tummy and speak in soothing tones.

"Every time you felt sick to your stomach, did you stop believing that your dad loved you?" I asked.

"Of course not."

"But you still needed his tender loving care—again," I pointed out. Then I asked, "If you could go back in time and get diagnosed with celiac disease early in childhood, instead of discovering it as an adult, and thus avoid all those tummy aches, but it would mean that you would miss out on all those times with your dad, would you do it?"

"As I look back," Jeff said thoughtfully, "those were some of my most tender memories from childhood." Then he teared up. "We lost my dad to emphysema four years ago, and I really miss him. I'll never have that time with him again. I wouldn't trade those experiences for anything."

Then Jeff looked over at Patricia. "Is that right? Is it really just that you want me to be attentive and comforting? Do you think we might eventually look back on these painful times as bonding moments, like they were between me and my dad?"

"Maybe. I don't know," Patricia said. "But I do need you to be patient and really listen to me. When your dad sat with you and rubbed your tummy, he didn't say, 'Isn't this all better yet? We just went through this yesterday and the day before. Isn't it enough for you to keep those times in mind today when it hurts?'"

LETTING HER HAVE HER FEELINGS

I recently overheard a conversation between one of my colleagues, Scott Peterson, and the wife of one of his clients who is being treated for a pornography habit. She seemed pleased with her husband's progress, so Scott asked her what was better now. What she *didn't* talk about was as significant to me as what she did. She didn't say, "It's such a relief that he's not looking at dirty pictures anymore" or "I'm so glad that he's not fantasizing about being with other women." A look of relief on her face, she said, "I'm free to talk with him about what I'm feeling now. It's so nice to be able to just be real with him. He used to get so out of sorts if things weren't just so, if I were upset, or if I didn't feel the way about things that he thought I should. He couldn't handle my emotions. Now I can just say it like it is. I don't feel like I have to walk on eggshells in the way I word things."

I recently talked with a couple who had, several years earlier, worked through issues related to the husband's pornography habit. Now that things were on a better track, they both said that their marriage was even better than it had been before. "Better than before you found out about the problem?" I asked.

"Yes," she answered, "and better now than it was before he even *had* a problem."

That may be difficult to imagine until we realize what a unique thing it is for men to really listen to and be with their wives when they feel emotionally raw. If working through how hurt our spouse feels about this problem can help us do better at that than we've ever done before, that's really saying something. Then perhaps it's not surprising that a wife would say that, all in all, she has no regrets. That she wouldn't go back and change anything. That she wouldn't trade what she has now, even though she's had to go through that hellish experience to attain it.

Married life is a minefield when the husband can't tolerate his wife's distress, when he takes her expressions of frustration as attacks and her complaints as criticisms. As he at first strains just to sit through discussions about his pornography problem and over time develops the ability to really listen to her feelings about it, he's training at the highest of high altitudes. A year down the road, when he comes home from work late, she will complain to him. Instead of taking it personally and getting mad or defensive or scarce, a man who has trained at high altitude will be able to really listen to how hard her day has been. He'll be able to see that it's not just—or even primarily—about him. She simply saved her distress up for him because he's her husband. Now he can see more clearly what a good thing that is—that it's him she wants to reach for when she's feeling bad. He'll be able to move toward her instead of fighting or fleeing. And she'll have the kind of man she really wants in her life.

Helping Her Purge Her Pain

It's perhaps the most common pattern we see among couples who are dealing with pornography issues: He is reluctant to talk about it—so much so that her opportunities to work through it by reaching out to him and talking out her feelings are stifled. Thus she's prevented from gaining more and more freedom over time from the issue of his pornography use. We've made sense of this pattern by exploring just how much of his world turns on how he's doing in her eyes. To delve into exactly how and how much she's been wounded and disappointed—for him to see the pain in her eyes and know that he's helped cause it—is terrifying and can seem, at a very primal and convincing level, like the exact wrong road to take.

However, giving her more opportunities to freely bring up and fully discuss her hurts is exactly the right road to take. Exploring her feelings deeply and thoroughly will ease her pain more in the long run than trying to just put them aside and hope they fade with time. Remember, if a man will open up and let into his ears and his head and his heart the feelings his wife shares, they can become like superglue between the couple. Negative feelings don't fester and grow when they're expressed and truly heard. Rather, each time, a little of their toxicity dissipates, a little of their flammability is defused. Miraculously, more and more, the husband, the one who has hurt her, becomes the toxicity dissipater and flammability diffuser of choice for her. What was once the wedge between the spouses becomes the Velcro.

The process of sharing her feelings and the tremendous healing that results does not occur in a moment or a day, but over weeks, months, and often years. Nonetheless, many couples find it helpful to have a "big talk" about her hurts and suffering and wounds and injuries to initiate this process or to catalyze it if it's already been occurring.

Men: Set aside adequate time—perhaps an hour or so—to talk in greater depth than usual. Use the questions we'll share later in this chapter to "interview" your wife. If needed, take more time a day or two later to have a second session to further discuss these questions and her answers to them.

Your goal is simply to listen—to truly hear what she says and then to empathize with how she seems to feel. Try to genuinely understand what your wife is going through: what she is experiencing now emotionally and what feelings she's been having that you have perhaps not fully understood or taken in. You may come into this discussion already feeling like you've had your wife's feelings regularly dumped on you as though out of a dump truck, since emotions have been so raw and abundant, and thus wonder, "How could I have possibly missed what she's feeling?" In truth, however, it may have been hard for you to take in her pain because you felt so ashamed at having caused it and were antsy to get those conversations over with. You may have been so eager to explain how the pornography meant something different to you than it did to her, to convince her that you're doing better now, to commit to avoid pornography in the future, and so on, that you neglected to first simply listen in an effort to understand. It usually takes a lot of reminding yourself to keep breathing (rather than holding your breath, eagerly waiting for it to be over) and trying to imagine what it has been like for her to have had those experiences she's had.

Most men feel a tremendous amount of pressure to respond verbally in a way that somehow helps. However, then they start to feel afraid they'll have the wrong response, or they feel self-conscious and sheepish that they don't feel worse, or perhaps they worry that their remorse may not be showing on their face. If this ends up being the case for you, don't give in to the temptation to end the discussion. Don't try to act the way you think she wants you to act—or even try to convey what you think she needs at first. Simply share with her that impulse. ("Gosh, it is hard to stick with this right now because I'm afraid you won't see the response in me that you want to see. I'm afraid this will disappoint you, that I'll be a disappointment to you again.") Then go back to listening and encourage her to continue to share her feelings. Your job is to keep her talking. She just needs you to be present, "there for her," and really hear her. That is doable, even if it feels threatening.

As a matter of fact, a sincere effort from an amateur listener will mean more to your partner than a perfectly timed textbook response from a professional. Genuine compassion and concern will radiate through even the most bumbled attempt at trying to provide emotional safety for your partner. Psychologist Robert Karen described this process when he said, "In love, you don't need to be rich, or smart, or talented; you just have to be there" (Karen 1990, 17).

Being there for your partner has nothing to do with perfection. Fixing the disconnection is what matters—even the willingness to try again. If the two of you end up in a moment where what you intended and what she heard are mismatched, then signal again. Try it a different way. Keep working to repair the mismatch until you can successfully reconnect with your partner's heart.

It helps to have this discussion sitting knee to knee or at least kitty-corner to each other so that she can look you in the eyes. Believe it or not, what she sees in your face will be much more powerful than anything she hears you say. It helps some men to take themselves out of the equation: "Even though this is about what I did that affected her, it's not about me anymore, it's about her—what she is going through. For the next hour and a half I don't have to apologize, convince her I'm contrite or that I'm going to do well in the future, or make amends . . . I just need to listen. She is the focus, not me or my behavior."

Women: It can be very helpful to your husband if—during this discussion, at least—you let him off the hook in the above regard. Remember that at this point, during the time you've set aside, he is not trying to say anything right or effective or helpful. His focus is not on saying anything at all, but on simply listening and trying to understand for a while. If he knows he'll need to respond, he'll probably be spending more energy thinking about how he's going to respond than taking in what is being said. Therefore, resist the impulse to demand a verbal response from him during this process. "So now that you see how badly I'm hurting, how can you just sit there and not respond? What in the world do you have to say for yourself?" Give both of you the gift of letting him remain free to receive what you're trying to convey.

QUESTIONS TO DISCUSS

Dr. Rory C. Reid, a research psychologist in the Department of Psychiatry and Biobehavioral Sciences at UCLA who has conducted numerous studies related to pornography use, has suggested several questions to help facilitate and deepen discussions between partners (see www.provocc.org). We've shared them with many couples in our practice and received feedback that quite often they really help get a dialogue rolling on a productive track. With his permission, we've listed these questions below:

- What has it been like for you to have the sacred trust you placed in me betrayed by my choices?
- How do you experience your days differently now than before the discovery of my behavior?
- What ongoing events or activities trigger painful feelings for you? How often do these experiences occur?
- How have my choices impacted your beliefs and feelings about intimacy in our relationship? What boundaries would you like to establish or change about intimacy?
- What fears do you currently have about me or our relationship? When are these fears more intense? Less intense? What helps reduce your fear? How do you physically experience fear (for example, bodily sensations, headaches, tension, restlessness, and so on)?
- What aspects of our relationship need to be reorganized in order for you to feel safer? What boundaries are you currently uncomfortable with?
- What things need to change in order for you to feel like you could begin to start trusting again?
- What aspects of my behavior were most offensive or painful for you?
- What aspects of this problem am I closed about? How do I shut you down from expressing your feelings? What is one thing I can do differently to help improve our discussions about difficult topics?
- To what extent do you feel trapped because of my choices? How can I help you feel like you have more options and choices?
- What impact have my choices had on spirituality in our home or in our relationship?
- As I work toward restoring trust in our relationship, what are some specific things I will need to pay attention

to? What things can I change that would give you some hope?

- What do you see as being the most important priority for our relationship at this time?
- In all that has happened, what has been the most painful aspect of your experience?
- What do you need most right now in our relationship?

Couples report feeling a mixture of both positive and difficult emotions after going through these questions. Consider the completion of this exercise as a significant step forward in the growth of your relationship. Discussing these questions requires courage on the part of both individuals. You're beginning something that is sure to trigger vulnerable feelings in both of you without knowing how it will end. Let the answers and feelings associated with these conversations settle on the relationship. If there are difficult feelings to sort out, feel free to give yourself permission to slow down and take time to absorb and process the emotions. Think of these questions as the beginning of a long conversation that won't be resolved quickly. Again, the goal isn't to check off a list of questions. The goal is to strengthen the bond by responding to a partner's distress and pain in a loving and supportive way.

• • •

As important as it is to repair the damage that has been caused to a marriage by pornography in the past, it's even more crucial for a husband to prevent relapse to his pornography habit so that healing wounds aren't reopened and relationship injuries aren't aggravated even further. The next two chapters will explore why people get stuck in a porn habit, why they stay stuck, and, more important, how they can get out—for good.

The next chapter explores the raw and emotionally vulnerable feelings that put people at risk of relapse. They have become con-ditioned, over time, to believe that what they need at such times is a sexual release, but it's not. They may *want* sex, but they *need* emotional closeness and support at such times. Chapter 6 is about men reaching out to their wives at such times instead of going back to porn. When it comes to actually meeting key emotional needs rather than just numbing them temporarily, when it comes to the emotional oxygen we all crave, pornography doesn't hold a candle to what a real relationship offers.

CHAPTER 5

The Feelings That Fuel Addiction

Women may have a hard time understanding why men are so vulnerable to the draw of pornography. That's part of why so many wives just can't leave the problem alone, can't get it out of their heads. It keeps troubling them: "I don't regularly fantasize about having sex with someone else. I thought he had the same values and commitment as I do. I thought he felt the same about me as I did about him. I thought fidelity to our vows was just as important to him as it was to me. He's a decent guy in so many other ways. Has he been faking that all this time? Are his apparent spirituality and religious devotion nothing but a ruse? How could he be what he seems and yet do what he's done?"

Helping Her Understand What Porn Does to You

It helps her to hear from you what was going on as you descended into a compulsive habit. Not so much about whether you prefer blondes or brunettes and what kind of tantalization (marketing by pornographers) you find irresistible. But it can help her to hear that you get tunnel vision just like an addict who is craving any other fix, which blocks out thoughts about faithfulness, family, and the values that usually guide your behavior. Perhaps most of all, it's helpful to hear why you were afraid to tell her about it. It's usually not, as most women fear, simply that you were afraid you would lose your access to pornography and your opportunity to view it once she knew about the habit. It's helpful for her to hear from you what your worst-case-scenario fears were.

As male counselors, we've found that some information we can bring to these discussions can also be helpful, although this territory can get dicey for us. When we talk about the physiological basis of male vulnerability to pornography addiction, it may come off like we're excusing bad behavior, which we don't mean to do. Despite that risk, we keep diving in because many wives find it helpful to understand some of the factors that may be influencing their husbands:

Men have a more robust dopamine response. Men were found to release higher levels of dopamine than women in response to the ingestion of amphetamines. Dopamine is a pleasure chemical in the brain that drives our "seek and satisfy" behavioral responses. Men's robust dopamine response may help account for why males have a higher incidence of addictive disorders (see www.reuniting .info).

Testosterone fuels sexual motivation. Males produce ten to twenty times more testosterone, on average, than women. Women receiving testosterone supplements find that their sex drive increases. In the words of one, "I found myself looking at men's body parts and thinking about sex at random times during the day. I always thought that I was living on a higher plane than my husband because that was the way he's always been about sex. Now I realize that it was more about hormonal differences than a gap in our spiritual maturity."

Even in the best of marriages, when testosterone levels between spouses differ, which is usually the case, it takes time to come to understand and honor each other's varying sexual desires and sensibilities. It's no secret, of course, that usually it's the man who has higher testosterone levels and a greater desire for sex, although some husbands and wives have roughly equal sex drives and in a minority of cases it's the wife who wishes they were more sexually active.

Regardless of how each spouse feels and what each prefers when it comes to sex, the important thing is to keep reaching out and opening up. When partners bring their differences *to* the relationship (instead of seeking outside outlets), they may each be challenged, but they keep growing together. As time goes on and differences in their drives and sensibilities continue to play out in various ways, those differences can enrich instead of diminish the relationship.

Our colleague Laura M. Brotherson, author of the book *And They Were Not Ashamed: Strengthening Marriage through Sexual Fulfillment,* works with many women who are shut down sexually for one reason or another. As she helps them awaken and embrace their sexuality, many report a whole new sense of aliveness and a more profound connection with their husbands. Once things are on a better track for the couple and sex has become mutually fulfilling and enjoyable, she often hears feedback like, "I really didn't understand what I was missing. Now I know!" "I felt broken and didn't know how to enjoy sex like I knew my husband did." "I used to think sex was carnal or dirty, but now I sense its deep spiritual importance." "I feel sad for all these years that I didn't 'get it.' I'm grateful my husband was so patient with me, and kept encouraging us toward something more."

As important as it is for a husband to respect and be genuinely touched by his wife's sensibilities about sex, it's equally important for her to respect his excitement about it, to truly allow it into her heart, not just try to "get what makes him tick" or even "be more accommodating." Male sexuality is not the problem. In fact, it can become a key (and enjoyable) part of the solution when he keeps pursuing her sexually in patient, loving ways and she keeps her heart open to all of her beloved, including his sexuality.

Sex is an extremely potent motivator for male primates. Researchers found an ingenious way to measure the motivation of rhesus monkeys. They offer them Berry Berry Juice in varying amounts, giving the monkey a choice between the juice and some other desirable object. The monkey may choose, for instance, to play with a ball when offered the choice between it and three ounces of juice. However, when offered enough juice, let's say five ounces, the monkey opts to go for the juice instead. In this way, the researchers created a hierarchy of priorities. These monkeys *liked* toys, but they *loved* the opportunity to gaze at a dominant member of their clan. However, nothing else held a candle to the biggest motivator of all: The monkeys rejected every offer of varying amounts of juice in exchange for the opportunity to keep gazing at the hindquarters of an estrus female monkey (Deaner et al. 2005).

How different are we as humans from rhesus monkeys? It's a question I ask audiences when I teach continuing education classes to other mental health professionals. Then I say, "Let's find out." On the screen is a PowerPoint slide to illustrate the study just described. I'm not sure if she's estrus or not, but there's a full-screen picture I managed to find on the Internet of the backside of a female monkey as she walks away from the camera on all fours. I walk back and stand beside a male in the audience, pull out a container of grape juice, and say, "This fourteen-ounce bottle of juice is all yours, but only if you're willing to stop looking at that picture." I've tried this in dozens of cities around the United States.

To the relief of every other male in the audience, every one of them has looked away from the screen.

Of course, this is the joke: We're different as humans . . . and yet not all that different as humans, by nature. We have the capacity like no other animal to subdue and tame our nature. None of the men I work with want to convince their wives they can't help themselves because they're just like animals. That's exactly what is worrying the women, and it's exactly what the men will work over time to eventually disprove. Nonetheless, these animal studies can help to some degree as we attempt to understand our vulnerability.

Men have a more powerful neurological response to porn. Researchers compared brain images of male and female subjects as they viewed erotic film excerpts. For the most part, both genders showed activation of corresponding brain regions. However, the men not only reported significantly higher levels of physiological arousal, they also, unlike the women, showed significant activation of the hypothalamus. As author Marnia Robinson explains it, it appears that pornography has the power to hijack a male brain's command center in a way it cannot in females (see www.reuniting.info).

In order to help women empathize a bit, I sometimes bring up another interesting piece of research. Scientists have discovered something that differentially affects women's brains, although not quite as powerfully as the degree to which erotica does men's. There is a substance that triggers a more robust response in the female hypothalamus compared to the male. So, what lights up women's potent "command center," this area of the brain that determines what rivets our attention and motivation versus what's ignorable? Any guesses about what that substance is? It's not cocaine. It's not heroin. It may be shopping, but that's not what the research measured. That's right, it's *chocolate.*

Of course, the physiological factors we've explored so far in this chapter represent just one small slice of the whole story. Not only is being male an incomplete explanation of the problem many men have with porn, it does absolutely nothing to suggest solutions. We'll always be men, just as our wives will always be women. She might be more vulnerable to an eating disorder because she's female, but acknowledging that would do nothing to help her overcome one. To have any hope of healing, we need to turn the discussion from our physiology to our feelings.

Most Relapses Are Brought on by Emotion

Sometimes addictive urges leave us alone. We can go various periods of time without the slightest hint of a problem. All's quiet. Looks like the coast is clear. Maybe we've got this problem licked once and for all. . . . Then suddenly, *Whammo!* Old cravings hit again, seemingly from out of the blue.

When we are just beginning our recovery—or are not yet in recovery—from addictive patterns, every day can be like setting out across a minefield. With each new day, each new week, each new month, there is the hazard of potential relapse. However, like the soldier walking through the minefield, we see no apparent signs indicating where the mines are located. We can be going along thinking everything's fine, and then suddenly we're back, caught up in a familiar primitive reaction.

One man put it this way: "I'd driven by that billboard dozens of times and it didn't even tweak me. Then, for some reason, that night, seeing that image up there had an awfully potent effect on me. I felt like Odysseus, trying to sail on past as the sirens sung out to me. I knew I was in trouble. 'Tie me to the mast! *Tie me to the mast!*' Why is it that I can do so well managing my thoughts for a time, to the point that I wonder whether I even have a problem anymore, and then suddenly be so vulnerable to that pull?"

I've spent many years being curious, sitting side-by-side with clients who were curious themselves, as we explored the nature of the dominoes in their lives that preceded their most potent cravings. We keep trying to trace the stream back. "There's the acting-out behavior. That's the dreaded waterfall you're trying to avoid. But what was going on right before you felt the strong pull at the cusp of the falls—the rapids above the waterfall, so to speak? Then, even earlier, the swift-running stream above the rapids? What was going on around and inside you? Then the slower-running stream before that? All the way back to the still waters, that point at which you last felt a sense of complete freedom?"

At first, doing this work, I thought we would be discovering an extremely broad range of assorted precursors. I didn't even know if it would be possible to develop an exhaustive list of vulnerability-heighteners because of the uniqueness of individual human beings and the vast potentiality of the human psyche. Nonetheless, I was hopeful that we might eventually amass a fairly comprehensive catalogue of triggers.

This process has become more exhilarating over the years, not because of the vast variety, but because of the profound similarity of the terrain above the falls in all of our lives. *For most of us, the urge to return to self-destructive behavior is usually most potent when we feel emotionally raw or unacceptable in some way or disconnected from someone important to us.* Consider the following examples. They're all things clients have told me they noticed once they started looking back at what was happening in the hours and days before they relapsed:

"I got home from helping the neighbor shovel snow off his sidewalk and it turns out Shelly was upset with me for leaving her to do the kids' bath and bedtime alone. I thought, 'No matter how hard I try I can't win.'"

"Another guy who'd been working as a temp alongside me was hired on permanently. I was down in the dumps about that."

"My stepdaughter was being so disrespectful and it seems like we may never be able to turn that around. I got thinking about her future and feeling like a failure as a dad."

"I saw an ad for one of my competitors. He's got three vans now and six or seven employees. I started comparing and feeling bad that our growth has plateaued."

"I was mad at Clara for spending so much money on having my shirts pressed at the dry cleaner. It felt like she wasn't respecting how tight our financial situation is and had ignored the concerns I tried to express to her about the need to cut back."

"I'd been in St. Louis five days and I knew I'd be there seven more. The training was interesting at first, but it was getting old. I'd seen the sights in town that I'd wanted to see. In the evenings, more and more, it was sinking in that I was alone there with very little to do. It left me feeling pretty empty inside."

WE HAVE A HARD TIME READING INNER SIGNALS

Some clients come into treatment having already made the connection between feeling bad and wanting to act out sexually. For many others, it's not apparent at first, or even for a while after they start looking for it. That's why addictions aren't overcome overnight; this process takes time and practice.

Part of the problem is that we get confused. We get our signals crossed. Research has shown that people who struggle with addictive cravings and compulsive urges are more likely than the average person to suffer from what psychologist and researcher Peter Sifneos calls alexithymia. The latin prefix *a-* means an absence or lack, *lexi* denotes language, and *thymos* refers to passion or emotion—in short, we have a hard time knowing what we're feeling and putting it into words. We have difficulty recognizing emotions for what they are, and so we naturally have a hard time expressing and effectively managing the visceral arousal associated with them. This leaves that energy charged within us, just waiting to be converted to addictive urges and cravings.

It's more challenging to identify what's going on inside us if we received feedback when we were younger that our feelings weren't important. One client, Kent, remembered a fishing trip he took as a child with his younger brother Kelly, his dad, and one of his dad's buddies, Rock. His dad had a short temper, so at first the kids didn't complain when they saw Dad pull out a six-pack of beer, peel the tab off one, and throw a can over to Rock. As the day wore on and the temperature rose, the kids kept wondering what they were going to drink. Kelly kept pleading to Kent in whispered tones, until eventually Kent finally approached his dad. "Me and Kelly are thirsty." Kent remembered that his father didn't even lift his gaze from the lake. "Adult beverages, son. You already know you can't have any."

Kent also recalled a family trip to see the dinosaur bones in eastern Utah. They were driving a particularly long leg of the trip. Once he felt like he wasn't going to be able to hold it any longer, he finally spoke up. "Dad, I have to go to the bathroom." His father's terse reply: "No, you don't."

Even as an adult, Kent got feedback that he'd better not trust his own feelings. When his business finally did well enough that he could afford the luxury car he'd always wanted, he called his dad to share the great news with him: "Guess what I just bought and am driving down the road in right now?" Then he had to hold the phone away from his ear, his dad's voice was so loud: "A BMW! Why'd you get a BMW? *Everyone* knows that Lexus makes a better car than BMW, son!"

I recall discussing in a group therapy session another client's recollection of elementary school portrait day. Chris had been excited to wear his favorite shirt—a multicolored striped knit turtleneck—for the pictures. "Oh, no, no, no," his mom said as he walked into the kitchen, ready to go. "We'll be sending a picture to Grandma, so you need to wear the red shirt she bought you for Christmas." Chris hated that shirt. It was a button-up Sunday shirt. And it was already too small for him. "So I put up a real stink," Chris recalled. "I did *not* want to wear that shirt."

"Hold it right there," I said to Chris as he was about to finish the story. "We'll pick it up at this point next week. If you have time, look through your keepsakes and see if you can find your school picture from that year."

The next week, Chris walked into our group session carrying a manila envelope. He pulled out an eight-by-ten glossy showing four rows of nine-year-olds with gap-toothed smiles decked out in bell-bottoms and fat-collared shirts. We gathered around and scanned the faces, looking for Chris's features in one of the kids. Immediately one of the group members yelped and pointed. Middle row, left side. First thing I saw was the long-sleeved red-velvet-chocolate-cake colored shirt, buttoned all the way up. There was young Chris's face gazing out at us from the photo, looking like he was being choked by a tight collar but attempting to smile nonetheless.

It's not that parents traumatize kids when they have them do something they don't like. Nothing's more common in childhood— even a healthy childhood—than being made to do things you'd rather not. The kind of squelching that leads individuals to suppress and eventually become ignorant of their inner signals is much more pervasive. It doesn't result merely from being made to wear a shirt one hates. In some cases, growing out of touch with one's feelings may have as much to do with the individual's reaction as with the way he or she has been treated. Maybe some kids fight through experiences that send the message to them that their feelings and wants are invalid; they manage to maintain a solid attunement to their inner reactions despite the flak they get when they assert themselves. Maybe vulnerable individuals simply care more about the feelings and reactions of others—which in moderation is certainly a desirable trait. Their conscientiousness leads them to put aside their own wants and needs and focus on pleasing others.

Individual differences might also play a role in other ways. It might be that some of us are less able to make sense of inner signals because of inborn differences in our capacity for processing our inner reactions and making sense of them. Although we may be influenced by experiences growing up to disconnect from our own emotions, there is also evidence that such differences are at least partially innate. Men are more prone to alexithymia than women, and some gender-based brain differences may help account for that.

Whatever the reason, it's a common trait among those who struggle with compulsive behavior: They have a hard time picking up and responding effectively to inner signals. They're cut off from their visceral selves. They learn to direct their attention elsewhere when they experience an unwieldy impulse or unwanted emotion. No wonder, then, that inner signals get crossed, and some people crave alcohol when fatigued, pursue sex when bereaved, or over-eat when they're actually lonely.

Beginning to Recognize and Allow Our Feelings

Much more important than understanding how and why we developed emotion blindness is learning how to overcome it. Here's how it started for Wayne. Four years into his marriage his wife discovered his pornography habit, and he became more motivated than ever to stop. They came in for counseling, and with my encouragement Wayne began paying more attention to how he felt in response to events and interactions with others in everyday life. At first he was convinced that he didn't feel as much as other people. He did; his feelings just weren't apparent. He was, as our colleague

Rod Jeppsen puts it, only hitting a handful of keys on the piano of emotions, instead of playing across the entire keyboard. Over time, subtle inner reactions became more clear to Wayne. He also could sense within himself an almost immediate imperative to dampen or dismiss what he felt, as though it weren't important. He made a point of trying to allow himself to feel whatever he was feeling.

One week Wayne and his wife, Megan, traveled out of state to spend time with his family at a yearly family gathering. One afternoon, after playing on the beach, a few of Wayne's nieces and nephews gathered around a TV set to watch a movie. As they looked at the options available, one of the boys saw a DVD of *Annie* and excitedly started talking about how much he liked it. Wayne's father said, "That's not a boy movie, that's a movie for girls." Megan and Wayne were sitting side by side on a nearby couch. Right after he heard his dad's comment, he felt Megan's fingers dig into his forearm. He looked up to see a pained look in her eyes. To that point he hadn't noticed a reaction within himself, but as he paid closer attention he noticed a distinct tightening in his chest—his breathing had suspended momentarily. Perhaps it was a sympathetic little gasp as he guessed that the boy might be feeling exposed and embarrassed. Then Wayne's nephew responded, "Nuh-uh, Grandpa. My friend Skyler likes it too, and he's a boy." Wayne felt an immediate lightening, like a fresh dose of oxygen had been let back into the room. *So this is what it's like to claim your feelings instead of stuffing them,* he thought.

In his life, Wayne had learned to squelch and deny emotional reactions in an effort to move on with life when he felt bad. It had become automatic. Then he had developed the habit of going to porn for some relief from the bad feelings that had built up. That little incident with the videos gave him a taste of how freeing it would be to acknowledge his feelings, use them as guides about what was needed, and express them more freely, as his nephew had done. He breathed an even bigger sigh as he considered what a relief it would be to be able to operate that way all the time in his life, to be free of the knot in his chest that he was beginning to recognize as an indicator that the feelings he was trying to ignore and move on from hadn't really gone anywhere.

Gerry Blasingame is a marriage and family counselor who specializes in treating developmentally disabled sex offenders. Imagine his challenge: He has to help individuals with extremely low IQs understand and overcome their sexual compulsivity. He has developed a model for explaining why we act out sexually that is brilliant in its simplicity (Blasingame 2001). He draws a ladder with several rungs. The top one is "Bad Sex Behavior." Can't get more straightforward than that. But we don't just find ourselves plopped there. We can only reach it from the rungs just below it. We have to prepare ourselves by fantasizing, planning, and, in the case of sex offenders, choosing and grooming a victim. However, we never get there, Blasingame insists, except by stepping up from solid ground by way of the first two rungs of the ladder. The bottom rung is "Feel Bad," and the one just above it is "Keep It to Myself." This is how we get from doing well to acting out: We feel bad, we keep it to ourselves, we look for or create an opportunity, and then we engage in bad sex behavior. My favorite thing about Blasingame's model is that the key to preventing relapse is equally simple. We can't avoid getting on that first rung of the ladder. As a part of life, we're going to feel bad, and it's likely to happen every day. The key is to avoid the second rung. Instead of keeping it to ourselves, we can start acknowledging when we feel bad and opening up to others about it.

CATCH RAW FEELINGS BEFORE THEY TURN INTO CRAVINGS

Roger was running fifteen minutes behind schedule. He sped along through the morning traffic, hoping he would hit all green lights, trying to make up at least some of that time. He was still feeling keyed up a couple of minutes later as he walked briskly through the side entrance of the nursing home where he worked. Vaughn, the center's physical therapist, was standing at the nurse's station as Roger passed. Vaughn looked up from the clipboard he was holding and gave Roger a wry smile. "Look who decided to finally show up for work," he said, and then with a flourish of movement he exposed his wristwatch and checked it with raised eyebrows.

To anyone watching, it would have seemed that Roger laughed the comment off as he continued down the hall, but he could feel the heat of the flush lingering on his face. Walking into his office, he was struck by how messy he'd left it. Binders were stacked and papers strewn on the desk. He thought of Vaughn's workspace: pads folded, balls all on the rack, belts hung in a row from longest to shortest. An empty feeling started in Roger's gut and swirled up to his throat—a mix of envy, shame, and frustration. He sat down and picked up one of the binders. His feelings seemed to settle and fade as his mind turned to his work, but a tightness in his chest lingered. Medical procedure codes and prices started to fill his mind, drawing his attention from the distress he'd just been feeling.

Then Roger caught himself. "Wait a minute. I can handle this differently. Nine months ago, this is the kind of experience to which I wouldn't have given a second thought." He sat back in his chair and took a deep breath. "I'm glad I know how important moments like this can be."

Roger had come to understand that he would set himself up for a greater risk of relapse to his addiction if he ignored strong feelings and tried to act like he wasn't fazed by events that impacted him emotionally. He had learned that simply acknowledging he was feeling something when he felt it was key. He'd been working on owning his emotional reaction, whatever it was. It was just a matter of being real with himself, settling in to whatever was going on inside, instead of mentally scrambling to get away from what he was feeling. He paused, stared at the wall, and tuned in. There was that yucky, pasty feeling in the pit of his gut. "I start to see myself as this bumbling loser," he thought. "My mind flips open the Rolodex that catalogs all of my weaknesses. Yep, that's what got kicked up just now."

Roger had also learned just how helpful it was to reach out to his wife, Peggy, at such times. He opened up his cell phone and sent her a text. "Feel bad over running late. Seems all my flaws pop into view. Wish I felt more on the ball." It wasn't long before he heard back from her: "Sorry you started the day feeling bad. Glad you reached out. You know I love you." That felt nice to Roger. His next breath was more relaxed and full. He could feel the tension of the morning dissipating a bit.

STIRRED-UP EMOTIONS DRIVE ADDICTION

It may seem to us like it "works" when we try to distract ourselves from distressing emotions, the way Roger used to. However, even when they're ignored, emotions continue to have a rousing effect on the body and brain. Feelings crank up the nervous system. That energy builds inside of us and needs some kind of outlet. Notice that the word *emotion* contains the word *motion*. This is exactly what feelings do: they move us. They create motion. It's impossible to keep an emotion from moving us. Once a feeling or an emotion activates, it begins to create movement throughout our whole system.

What happens to this visceral arousal? Where does the energy from stirred-up, unacknowledged emotion go? How does it move us? In what direction does it take us? For many of us, it fuels compulsive urges and cravings. This conclusion is supported by some interesting research on compulsivity.

In one study (White 1973), two groups were invited to showings of several movies. A group of average-weight female college students were shown what the researchers considered to be an emotionally neutral movie: a travelogue of India. When the movie ended, they were invited to enjoy the snacks at the back of the room before leaving. After the students all left, the researchers weighed the snack trays to figure out the average number of ounces consumed by each woman.

A second group, made up of overweight students, were shown the same movie and offered the same spread of treats. Once again, the trays were weighed and calculations made. The researchers discovered that the average number of ounces consumed was virtually the same for the women in each of the groups. That was a bit surprising: even when they were offered an abundance of snacks, the compulsive eaters showed the same restraint as the other women.

The researchers didn't stop there. They invited both groups in to watch another movie. This time it was *An Officer and a Gentleman*. If you've seen the movie, you may remember how you felt when Richard Gere's character, finally a naval officer, swept Deborah Winger's character into his arms and carried her out of the factory where she worked. One of Hollywood's most emotion-packed endings. Credits rolled. Again, for the college women, there were treats. The average women ate about the same amount they had after watching the travelogue. But after the next showing, when the overweight women left the room and the researchers went back to complete their measurements and calculations, they didn't need a scale. The trays had been cleared entirely.

The implications of this research are clear: If we've struggled with compulsive or addictive behavior, we're more prone to relapse in an emotionally charged state.

ACKNOWLEDGING EMOTIONS HELPS US
KEEP OUR MENTAL CLARITY

Simply owning our emotional reactions—recognizing that we're feeling something when we're feeling it—goes a long way toward preventing relapse to addiction. Unacknowledged feelings remain generic energy that can more easily be given another label and converted into an impulse to relapse.

University of Illinois researchers Norbert Schwarz and Gerald Clore phoned Chicago residents and asked them to rate their sense of well-being and satisfaction in a variety of areas of life (Schwarz and Clore 1983). Perhaps it's not surprising that those who were interviewed on sunny days rated themselves as being more satisfied and better off than those who were interviewed on rainy days. It's easy to understand why the weather might affect our mood, which in turn might affect the way we feel about other things. Nonetheless, in everyday life, most of us are not aware of the effect that mood-altering factors have on our decision making. Stirred-up emotional energy can color our perception of everything, regardless of how those emotions got stirred up. As we move through our day, it's easy to forget the energy's origin, especially if we tried to suppress our reaction and move quickly past the negative feelings. Plus, we get caught up in the other things in our lives that we're seeing through now-tinted lenses. We assume that it's the mayor's job performance that makes us so annoyed with him we want to throw the bum out of office. We suppose that it's our coworker's failure to do her fair share of work on the project that has us feeling disgruntled. And, most dangerous of all, we conclude that we're out of sorts because it's been so long since we've had a fix and we're really craving what our addiction has to offer.

Although it's easy to miss the factors that influence our emotion and color our perception, it's also possible to correctly

identify them. Once we do, there's genuine power in that awareness. Simply seeing the factors that trigger emotional reactivity
can diminish their influence. In the weather study just described,
a second round of subjects were asked an additional question at
the beginning of the interview, before they started rating aspects
of their lives: "How's the weather in Chicago today?" (The inter-
viewer was calling from another city.) After answering that single
question, those subjects who were phoned on rainy days rated
themselves as being just as happy and satisfied with their lives and
the mayor's job performance as those who were phoned on sunny
days. Their mood may not have improved, but once it was attributed to the weather it had no effect on their judgments about other
things. Once influences on our emotional state are nailed down,
made conscious, and put into words, they are no longer convertible and transferable.

This skill of identifying the previously unconscious influences
that can impact well-being and impair decision making was applied
to help addicts free themselves long before Schwarz and Clore
did their research. Starting in 1943 a group of recovering alcoholics sat together in a small room in St. Catherine's hospital talking
about what they were learning about factors that increased their
risk of drinking. We can imagine their conversation: "When my
wife and I get into a fight, I'm more vulnerable." "Going on a business trip by myself is like walking through a minefield." "If I try to
go without lunch, instead of feeling like I'm starving later in the
day, I feel like I need a drink." "I struggle more when I'm beat and
need some rest."

As they looked for and talked about the slippery slopes of
their everyday lives, they discovered that it wasn't just the craving of alcohol or the urge to drink that they had to watch out
for. These early members of what we now know as Alcoholics
Anonymous were finding that if they didn't take care of themselves

nutritionally—if they deprived themselves of food or went too long between meals—they were more at risk of consuming alcohol. If they harbored resentments, lost their temper, or worked themselves into a fit of anger about something, they were more at risk of drinking. Not only that, but if they felt isolated, as if they had no support, and spent too much time alone instead of around other people, they were more likely to get intoxicated. And finally, when they were worn out from working too hard or not getting enough rest or sleep, when fatigue got the best of them, they were more likely to take a what? A nap? No, a *drink!*

In other words, these increasingly wise members of this budding fellowship were developing a detailed map not only of the catastrophic hazard—drinking—but of the inner precursors that surrounded and led up to it. They simplified their observations to a point where they could be easily recalled them later. They used the mnemonic H.A.L.T. to remind themselves and each other not to get too hungry, angry, lonely, or tired—or if they did (after all, these are naturally and regularly occurring states in our lives), at least they might remember that they were in a slippery zone. The H.A.L.T. mnemonic was a handle to hold on to, helping them assess and differentiate the cloudy, swirling motivational undercurrents that tugged and pulled and pushed at them in the heat of impulsive moments when things could otherwise seem completely overwhelming, chaotic, and confusing.

We can imagine the first few times when fellowship members said, "Instead of going to the bar, why don't I lie down for a nap?" or, "Maybe I just need to get a bite to eat." Confusing different drives and needs may sound silly when we're in a calm, rational state, but in the heat of the moment it's a trap we fall into quickly and automatically unless we remind ourselves to tune in to other inner signals besides the impulse to pursue addictive behavior. As we cue ourselves to turn our attention inward when we experience a craving, we set ourselves up for those aha moments when what was right there all along finally becomes apparent.

When we are progressing in our recovery, everyday life is no longer like trekking across an unmarked minefield. Instead, because of the work we've done to identify our emotions and other inner signals, we have an increasingly detailed map of the terrain we're traversing. We come to see the areas of the terrain that slope down toward the mines on the minefield. Instead of just avoiding the mines themselves, we avoid the slopes around them, lest we get there and discover that they're particularly slippery today. Or, if we do decide to take a path that puts us anywhere in the vicinity of what might be an active mine, we make the necessary preparations and take the precautions that are prudent. Rather than increasing the likelihood of relapse, our feelings can provide guidance and motivation for our journey.

Once we see them for what they are, our feelings (and other inner signals like hunger and fatigue) can remain what they are: signals that we need something. Then we can seek what is genuinely needed, so that the need doesn't remain unaddressed and unfulfilled, leaving the energy within us revved-up and ready to stoke our appetite for sex or some other potentially addictive behavior.

Developing the Ability to Stay with Our Emotions

When Gene and his wife, Dana, came to our clinic for a day of intensive therapy, they'd already explored in treatment why it was hard for him to deal with her when she was upset. Some of it went back to his childhood. As a child, Gene had experienced a sense of deprivation and helplessness watching his mother deteriorate physically as her lupus progressed. Before that, Gene had remembered his mom as a bright and energetic woman who had always been there for him when he was in need. As she got sicker, she stayed at home in bed more and more of the time. Her emotional distress also became more apparent. Gene could tell that she was getting sicker and sadder as time wore on, and he would do everything he could for her when his dad wasn't home. He'd prop her pillow. He'd rub her feet when it wasn't too painful. He'd bring her water in her big plastic mug, half full of ice just the way she liked it. Even though he was only seven at the time, he even learned to cook her up some scrambled eggs when she needed a snack and wanted something warm.

No matter how hard he tried, of course, Gene could never make things all better for her. He loved the way her eyes lit up as she told a visitor about what a good helper he was. He loved it when she took a minute to look deep in his eyes as she ruffled his hair or held her hand on his cheek. He hated it when she still cried even after he'd done everything he could think of. A part of him felt wrong about spending more and more time away from home as he grew into his teenage years. It was a relief to him to stay busy and involved in soccer practice and games, to be out doing things with friends, and out with girls once he started dating. Nonetheless, he had lingering feelings of guilt that Mom was home alone and in pain, and he wouldn't be there for her if she needed anything.

Now Gene was in his mid-forties. He had become an investment advisor, and he loved it when he could help clients calm down after they'd called in distress over a drop in a stock price or feel good again after he'd helped them rearrange their investment portfolio. Friends, neighbors, and extended family members came to him for help because they appreciated how patient and understanding he was.

Too often, unfortunately, Dana got a different version of Gene. For instance, she had lost her temper when asking him to straighten up the storage room in their basement. He'd dumped his camping gear there when he'd gotten back from a trip a week earlier. She had felt bad about getting mad and had apologized later, but for weeks after that he was demeaning and sarcastic whenever he found her shoes in the living room or dishes left in the sink overnight. She winced at one of his biting comments and asked Gene why he was being so uptight about things. "You're the one who seems to need this place perfectly tidy!" he retorted.

If Dana ever got stern with the kids, things seemed to deteriorate really quickly between them as a couple. Once she scolded their thirteen-year-old daughter for slacking in her piano practice. When the girl started crying, Gene said to her, "Don't let it get to you, honey. Your mom's just on one today." Then as he walked out of the room past Dana he growled under his breath, "I guess we can't all be as perfect as you are, can we?"

"He is so empathetic with others," Dana asked as she sat with him in my office. "Why does he care so little about me?"

I had talked with Gene individually, so I knew what was going on for him at such times. "Oh, it's not that he doesn't care," I said, "although I agree that his behavior can be very rude. It's that the stakes are so high with you. He cares so much about how things are going between the two of you that he gets a little crazy inside if he feels like he's lost esteem in your eyes. His world goes bleak, the wind is out of his sails, he feels defeated and deflated."

Earlier in their marriage, Gene had acted out sexually when he felt at odds with Dana. Over the last few years, in part perhaps due to the threat of the loss of his marriage, he had avoided such behaviors. Nonetheless, he was still acting out, in a sense, in that he would lash out at her when he felt strong emotions, particularly feelings of shame. I knew that if his marriage was going to thrive, he had to learn to respond differently at such moments.

"I know I can overreact and I need to change how I respond at times like those," Gene said, "but how do I keep from feeling so crappy inside when she's critical or it feels like she's being too harsh? I hate that feeling. Something's not right, she's upset about it, and it seems like she could let it go but she's choosing to make it a big deal. Everything can be going smoothly and it seems like she just has to find something that doesn't sit right with her and make everyone else miserable about it. That's what it seems like to me at the time, anyway. How do I get myself to not be so bugged by that?"

Gene's questions exposed the fatal error in his thinking. He was asking, "How do I keep from feeling crappy? How do I get myself to not be bugged?" This was the misguided perspective that was keeping him stuck: He thought he could discover a way to avoid feeling bad, avoid getting bothered. Remember Blasingame's ladder to acting out: The first rung is "feel bad." It's a rung, a place in life, we can never avoid. Gene had always wanted a way out of feeling bad as a kid when his mom was sick and struggling. He had worked at it diligently, and yet the pain was unremitting, physically for his mom and emotionally for both of them.

Now, Gene hated it when something in his relationship made him feel bad. It was the pain of discord with Dana that he had often sought relief from by consuming pornography. These days, he was abstaining from that habit but was still pursuing another pattern, a habitual way of relating to Dana, in an effort to avoid pain. He kept sending the message to her that strong negative feelings were unacceptable. Whenever she expressed disapproval, he argued and made rude comments and put her down, as though he was trying to punish her out of expressing dissatisfaction. It was as though he was saying to her, "I can't stand seeing you unhappy with me or the kids. So you need to knock it off."

We couldn't help Gene not feel bad, but we could help him deal differently with the terrible feelings that swamped him when he could tell that he had let Dana down or disappointed her in some way. You've probably heard the saying, "I love you, not just for who you are, but for who I am when I'm with you." Its complement is also true: "I get upset, not so much for who you are, but for who I am when I'm with you." I asked Gene to think about it: "When Dana's upset, what do you become, what place do you go to emotionally, that you have such a hard time tolerating? How do you start to see yourself that makes you so uncomfortable? What do you want the most and fear the most at those times?"

I encouraged him to sit with the feelings that came up at such moments instead of trying to scramble away from them by attacking Dana. I suggested he patiently stay with the feelings, remember to take nice, full breaths, and pay attention to what was happening in his body. Then, after buying a little time and space, he could talk to Dana in a different way about the feelings that were there. Gene started to become more aware of the tender feelings that led him to lash out. When he brought them to Dana in their more basic, tender form, she was much more able to respond in a supportive way.

For instance, a few weeks later, in the middle of a five-hour drive to visit Dana's sister and her family in Boise, Idaho, she became uncomfortable with how long Gene would take his eyes off the road to look at the scenery. "I'm getting worried that you're not paying enough attention to your driving," she said to him.

Later, when he told me about it, Gene said, "At that moment it was like a kick in the gut. It was hard to keep breathing, even though you've kept beating that into my head. I could hear your voice, 'Breathe, Gene, breathe!' It was literally like the wind had been knocked out of me. Everything I'd done to prepare for the trip seemed like wasted effort. That I had changed the oil and checked the tire inflation and had been driving for three hours seemed like it meant nothing to her if she was going to criticize me for glancing away from the road. And if it meant nothing to her, it was certainly useless to me. There was a part of me that felt like turning around and driving back home. It was like, if I couldn't please her, this little family vacation was not even worth taking. In fact, life was drained of its purpose. I might as well pull over on the side of the road, get out, have her drive off without me, and I could just sit there, not eat or drink anything, eventually just die, and rot there until I'm a pile of bones on the side of the road. It feels like I'm overdramatizing to say it that way, but that actually captures pretty accurately the way I get feeling in those moments. So, to sit with that crappy feeling as I drove was very difficult. Eventually I could get a little more air, and I paid attention to where I was feeling it physically. As usual, it was like a hundred-pound weight on my chest. Heaviness in my heart area and even my shoulders."

When they pulled off in Burley, Idaho, for a break, Gene asked Dana to take a little walk with him away from the car and the kids.

"It probably would have seemed like I was overreacting if I'd pulled over back there and said you could drive the rest of the trip."

Dana's eyes widened expectantly. "Well, yeah . . ." she said tentatively.

"But it's funny how desperate I get feeling when it seems like things take a sudden drop after it's been smooth and ideal between us. I discover that you feel like I'm not performing up to snuff, and suddenly I want to abandon all efforts and get away from you. Get off the playing field altogether and out of the spotlight so that I don't have to deal with how bad it feels to disappoint you. That's how much our relationship means to me, how much you mean to me, and how much I look to you for feedback about whether I'm doing well or not."

"Oh, honey, I had no idea that comment would pull the rug out from under you that way. I'm sorry you ended up feeling so bad. I didn't even realize you were feeling bad." Then she laughed. "A few months ago there would have been no doubt that I'd stepped on your toes because you would have stomped back on my entire foot. Now I'll have to keep my eye out for that more. I don't want to hurt your feelings." She gave him a hug.

"I may have been overreacting when I said that about your driving," Dana continued. "I felt the Suburban jerk a little when you corrected and got back into your lane one time and so then I started watching you for a minute. When I saw you looking at the scenery, I thought, 'Does he remember we're here with him?' You know how I get panicky when I think that we might not be your first priority. That's when I get feeling shaky inside. Is it possible that something else, even the roadside scenery, might come before our safety? Logically I know it isn't, but that thought enters my mind and I can't stand it. Then it seems like I can't help but let you know how I'm feeling in hopes that you'll show me you do care. And it worked. I felt more secure after that with your driving. I guess I need to convey that more, on the positive end, how safe and secure you make me feel when I know that what's important to me is important to you. It means everything to me."

She squeezed Gene again, tighter this time. "It made the drive so nice. So much so that I didn't realize you were stewing and hurting over there. You really do make me feel happy and secure. I love the way you take care of me and our family."

As they got back in the car, Dana turned back to the kids. "Everyone say thanks to Dad for the Corn Nuts and soda."

"Thanks, Dad!" the chorus came back.

"And let him know how much we appreciate him getting us up to Linda and Kevin's safely."

Gene knew it was set up, so it surprised him how much it warmed his heart when his three-year-old said, "Youwa gweat dwiva, Dad!"

The Richness of Men's Emotional Lives

It's become cliché, the idea that men are not emotional. Men are often the punch line for relationship jokes because of how unemotional and disconnected they sometimes appear. In our experience, however, men are highly emotional. It's just that they have so much working against their being able to process and regulate emotion in a healthy way.

Novelist Pat Conroy described a man's hidden emotional experience this way: "I could feel the tears within me, undiscovered and untouched in their inland sea. Those tears had been with me always. I thought that at birth, American men are allowed just as many tears as American women. But because we are forbidden to shed them, we die long before women do, with our hearts exploding or our blood pressure rising or our livers eaten away by [addiction] because that lake of grief inside us has no outlet. We, men, die because our faces were not watered enough" (Conroy 2002, 216).

One of the most painful experiences for a man is to be viewed as weak. When a man is faced with a situation in which he is powerless to respond, he will often resort to aggression or withdrawal in order to save face. Traditional "boy-code," as Dr. William Pollack describes it, prevents men from admitting their feelings of vulnerability and insecurity. Many men were faced with situations as children or teenagers when they failed at something and experienced humiliation. As a result, these men will do virtually anything to avoid appearing weak or vulnerable (Pollack 1998, 6).

Psychologist David Wexler put it well when he said: "A shamed boy becomes a hypersensitive man, his radar always finely tuned to the possibility of humiliation. His reaction to slights—perceived or real—and his ever-vigilant attempts to ward them off can become a kind of phobia. Tragically, the very men who are most desperate for affection and approval are the ones who usually can't ask for it; instead, they project blame and rejection and perceive the worst in others" (Wexler 2010, 22).

When a man who has betrayed the trust of his wife by viewing pornography sees the look of fear and disappointment in his wife's face, he will experience her distress as physiologically and emotionally punishing. This isn't because he's just a big jerk. Actually, it comes from a deep emotional part of him that needs her approval and acceptance so badly that he gets overwhelmed emotionally (and then physically) and has to do something to deal with the terrible cascade of intensity.

Most men were never taught how to recognize or deal with these emotional surges, which every man has experienced at some point in his life. These experiences can surprise men so much that they often will resort to unhealthy and relationship-unfriendly tactics to get out of the discomfort. In cases of pornography use, reaching out to the soothing comfort of sexual relief becomes the emotional regulator, often beginning when the user is a young man.

The good news is that the source of pain is also the source of healing. As a man begins to understand his own emotions, which include the negative experience of shame and failure, he can use that same pain to not only rebuild trust in his relationship with his partner but also soothe his wounded masculinity.

For example, as his wife is talking to him about how rotten it feels to be betrayed and humiliated by his pornography use, he might see that his pain in listening to her is coming from his failure to protect her. Instead of attacking her, which would violate his deepest desire to protect her, he could continue listening, do some deep breathing while she's talking, and take her feelings seriously. As he hears her and lets her have a voice about how she feels, he's offering her protection. Although it is painful for him to experience his wife's distress, as he allows the protective part of him to rise up and comfort his wife, they will both experience relief from the damaged bond.

Dealing Differently with the Feelings That Fuel Addiction

Lance looked tenser than usual when I met with him that April morning. "I'm under a ton of pressure because my boss was in town," he said. He worked as the regional manager for an international manufacturing company. "But so far, so good," he said with a sigh. "His stay has gone well, so far. I'm so relieved. I'm not going to lose my job." His company was so aggressive, he explained, that sometimes they would make wholesale changes in local leadership—fire the entire management team—just to "shake things up" if they didn't like the way things were going. "Yeah, his stay is going well so far," Lance said, "but I know I'm going to want to go to porn as soon as he leaves."

"This is perfect timing, then," I told him, "a great chance for you to explore and stay in touch with all of the strong feelings that drive your addiction." He committed to track them and try to stay with them rather than trying to distract himself from them.

The next time we met he reported, "I sometimes feel like a glass house. Like one comment from the CEO is all it would take and I'd shatter. I never portray that to my team. They'd never suspect it, I'm sure. But inside, I feel like I could fall apart. I don't know why I'm so insecure. For some reason I crave those votes of confidence or pats on the back from corporate. That kind of recognition would go a long way, but of course I'll never get it—it's just not that kind of company."

Once again I encouraged Lance to neither distract himself, even with seemingly innocent distractions, nor try to run from his emotions. "Stay with that sense of insecurity, that vulnerability of feeling like you might shatter or completely fall apart."

Next time we met, he said, "This week I fell apart. All of my emotions were close to the surface. I feel like I'm worthless, I don't amount to much. There's just not a lot of worth to me." Lance wasn't in tears, but his eyes were bloodshot. "I felt like going fetal: sitting in a corner and rocking. I felt utter despair, and it was enormous. It just encompassed me and it was hard for me to see a way out." Of course, his tried-and-true way out was pornography. "I think I'm tasting the depths of what I've been running from by lapsing to sexual titillation and stimulation. All of this was masked very effectively by that . . . well," he corrected himself, "maybe not effectively, but at least temporarily. Now," he worried aloud, "how am I going to deal with these emotions?"

"It's not something you're *going to do*," I responded. "You're already doing it."

"Oh, my," he snorted a strained laugh, "so this is healing?"

"But you don't have to suffer alone," I suggested.

"I'm too embarrassed to talk about it to Gina," he said, wide-eyed. "I don't want my wife to know I feel like a loser, a wacko guy who has no self-esteem."

"If she were struggling in this way," I asked, "how would you feel if she were just gutting it out on her own? What if she worried so much about what you'd think of her that it kept her from coming to you?"

I was doing everything I could to sway Lance because I'm convinced that it's not just soothing to share our feelings with loved ones—we actually become even more aware of what we're feeling when we open up to those we love. We become more real than we are at any other time, and more in touch with who we are deep down, when we're around our primary attachment figure. Plus it deepens our bond with them. This is just the opposite of how we detach from our emotions and everything else that makes us real when we zone out, isolate, and reach for our addiction. The first path cultivates connection within and connection between; the other breeds disconnection on both fronts.

The following week Lance reported, "I usually want to be quiet and alone when I'm feeling bad. I talked anyway." He shot me a dubious glance. "It was hard not to cry. I feel like a bigger doofus. I don't want to expose that part of myself. I don't even like looking at it. I don't want her to realize I have these scary deep thoughts I don't know how to deal with. It's the opposite of what I want to be for her. In the longer run, later in the week, I guess I felt better. During: I didn't like it; after: there was some relief. But I really don't want it to be difficult for her, for her to have the same doubts I do. I want to protect her. I've worried that she'll lose confidence in my ability as a breadwinner."

Lance noticed that Gina actually seemed more relaxed and happier over the next few days. One night, she was doubled over laughing as she described to Lance—and then even demonstrated—the trampoline moves of their two-year-old and four-year-old from earlier that day. Then she collapsed onto the bed and sat face-to-face with him. She looked him in the eyes, holding his gaze longer than usual in silence. Then she sighed and nuzzled into a relaxed embrace.

Lance experienced periods of relief over the next several weeks, but the immense emotional pain he'd been feeling kept recurring. "It gets so bad, I sometimes wonder why I'm trying. Over the last few days I've been questioning, what am I doing that's adding any value? At work, with my family? I might as well not be here. I went to Gina and talked out what I was feeling; I didn't 'act out' with the pornography. Surprisingly, even though she was out of town and we only talked on the phone, I didn't feel a tremendous pull to go to that stuff. Normally I would have been lying there in bed alone, unable to sleep, and finally would have concluded that I might as well go look at some stuff."

A couple of weeks later Gina was taking Lance's jacket to the dry cleaners and discovered two hotel keys in the breast pocket. She showed him the keys and asked him about them. He shrugged. "They must have been from my trip to the home office in Milwaukee a couple of months ago," he guessed.

Gina's shoulders relaxed as she sighed, "I figured it was probably something like that. But even if just for a brief moment, there was that fear that you're going to dump me. That you just might be having a relationship with someone else."

As he described how she had cried in his arms, Lance commented about how his own disclosure of emotions seemed to opened the door for Gina to share more of what was going on inside for her. "I'm more attuned to her, and she senses it. She says I feel softer," Lance laughed, "and that is exactly what I was initially afraid of becoming. I didn't want to be that needy, overly whiny, 'What about Bob?' guy who can't get anything done. I didn't want to freak her out by crying in front of her. I felt like I was too emotional, too much of a drain. I was miserable and I didn't want to drag her into the cesspool with me. For a while, even after I was making it a habit to open up to her, I kept wondering, 'Where's the peace in *this?*'"

Lance paused and leaned back in his chair. "Work is still a mess. I don't feel peace there, and maybe I never will for as long as I work for this company. But I do have this deeper sense, more and more of the time now, that things always work out. There will be hard times, but we just need to persevere, be grateful for the things that really matter—especially our family."

The following week Lance said, "I was feeling the usual. Work was eating me up. I was afraid I'd lose my job. It was almost embarrassing, but I came home and said, 'I want to be held.' Gina was good enough about it. She tries to be open to it. I said, 'I need more of this than I let on. I need you more than you realize.' It felt weak to say that. Our CEO never needs anybody. It feels like I need to be more like him. Of course, he's been through three marriages and his daughter in drug rehab won't take his calls. But somehow it seems like I should stay tough and self-sufficient all the time, like he seems to."

Lance smiled. "I said it felt weak, but that feeling's fading. Now there's a bigger part of me that drinks it in. I relish her embrace at the end of the day, her soothing voice. I used to think that she just wasn't the nurturing type of person. She could be, with the kids, but she wasn't a very encouraging wife. I saw her mom be a nurturer, but I concluded that she must not have gotten that gene from her mother. Well, what do you know: She's wonderful at it. I was just so closed off emotionally that she hadn't ever realized that I needed it. She thought I was the self-assured guy I wanted to be, even though inside I was dying."

The last time I met with him in person, Lance told me about an experience with his daughter. She was crying about having to practice the piano. "It was the kind of thing that might have set me off before. I'd have freaked out: 'Go to your room! This is ridiculous! We've spent all this money on lessons! Gina, why do we bother when it turns into such a drama?'" This time he let his daughter talk out her feelings about playing the piano. She had already missed two days earlier in the week. Her recital was in two weeks. The new piece she was learning seemed too hard. It was hard to hold her fingers right, and her teacher got mad if she lowered her hands. "Uh-huh," he said to her several times as she talked, his hand on her shoulder. "It's tough," he said after it seemed that she had cataloged all of her complaints. "I know it's hard, but come back and do it." He quietly walked out, wondering how she would respond. A couple of minutes later he heard the halting sounds of *Claire de Lune* coming from the living room again.

Several months later, when I followed up with Lance by phone, he said that things had continued to go well in his recovery and in his marriage. He attributed a rising threshold for avoiding inappropriate outside sexual temptation to their improved relationship as a couple. "When we start to talk at night and I unload, I get finished with what I was planning to talk about and then I often say, 'I guess I've also been dealing with this other thing. And also what do you think about this issue? And I was frustrated about such and such.' We thrive on connecting and neither of us wants to stop." He continued, "When I am tempted, I look for the emotional charges. Once I realize them, I honor them even if they seem silly. Every day, regardless of whether I'm tempted or not, I fish around for tender feelings just to keep tabs on them. Those are the things I open up to Gina about at the end of the day. And those discussions are my little oasis from daily life, a little slice of heaven." Before we hung up, I asked him whether Gina shared her feelings during those talks. "The other day her friend had some flowers delivered—a gift from her husband. That night Gina said, 'I'm not saying this to put you on a guilt trip. I don't want you to feel bad. But my heart stopped for a minute and I thought, *I'll never have that. Lance is so practical, he's just not a flower kind of guy.* It's not the flowers themselves, but what it would mean to me to know that you felt that strongly about me. That you thought about me even when you didn't have to. I want to feel that important to you.' Then she told me the next night, 'The flowers you sent me this afternoon were wonderful, honey, they made my day . . . but it meant even more to me the way you listened last night to what flowers would mean to me without getting defensive.' So, yeah," Lance concluded, "she's opening up and sharing her feelings. She'll also let me know if she sees something on a TV talk show about pornography that gets her worrying or brings back painful memories."

Emotions have the potential to drive a great deal of unhealthy behavior, which can in turn lead to untold and unnecessary suffering. But that can't happen once those feelings are talked out the way Lance and Gina had learned to do. Once strong feelings come out into the open in the intimate space between a committed couple, they turn from potentially toxic to potently enriching. If we remain open to our own and our spouse's feelings instead of hiding, judging, solving, or getting defensive, they become that superglue that can help bond us together as inseparable partners.

PRACTICE RECOGNIZING AND SHARING FEELINGS

Emotions in our lives are like the spotlights in a stage show: They guide our gaze, telling us which parts of the drama are most important. They give us focal points so that we don't need to take in the entire stage. Yet, even as they color our experience, they do so stealthily, leaving us unaware of their operation. They *direct* our attention most powerfully because they do so without *drawing* our attention.

If we always enjoyed the show, perhaps we would never have to pay much attention to our feelings. However, our emotions don't always operate adaptively. Our worst habits are often driven by emotions. The ways we act in response to powerful, recurring emotions are often self-defeating and detrimental to ourselves and our relationships.

Fortunately, we can diminish the potential of emotions to hijack our minds and wreak havoc in our lives. We begin to do so by turning our attention to our feelings and focusing on the very internal processes that once only captured and directed our attention—sort of like turning our gaze away from the action on stage and watching the spotlight technician during a play. As we become more aware of our emotions, we gain an ability to choose how we want to act in response to them. They can remain a rich and important part of our lives without dominating our experience and dictating our behavior. In fact, when we tune in to them attentively and patiently, they become a constructive force, operating to motivate us, guide us, and strengthen our connection to those we care about.

The practice of regularly identifying and expressing feelings is a great way for us to deepen our awareness of emotions. As an experiment, for the next couple of weeks use the canned statements below to direct your attention to subtle feelings and prime discussions with your spouse. This method is artificial and thus not likely to be useful long term, but I've seen it help many people get the process started. If you're not ready to check in with your spouse, start by writing out your responses in some kind of journal. Simply read the following incomplete sentences and fill in the blanks. The wording of the sentences is designed to help you become more accepting of the entire range of your feelings and own the kind of feelings that you might usually suppress, reject, or dismiss. You want to develop the ability to come to terms with all of your feelings, not just the ones you view as acceptable or mature.

- "It probably shouldn't have bothered me, but today when _____, I felt _____."
- "It seems all wrong that I felt this way, but _____."
- "I feel sort of pathetic saying it, but today when _____, I felt _____."
- "I feel foolish for reacting this way inside, but today when _____, I _____."
- "It feels silly to even want or need this, but today I would have liked _____."
- "It seems like I shouldn't feel this way, but _____."
- "It's just a little thing, but today when _____, I felt _____."

- "I feel wimpy for saying it, but today I felt _____
  when _____."

- "I felt insecure today when _____."

- "I felt vulnerable today when _____."

- "I felt childish or immature today when _____."

Notice what happens as you begin to give a voice to these previously unacknowledged emotions. Pay particular attention to the changes in your physical body—especially your chest and gut—after going through this exercise. Since unacknowledged feelings aren't granted full expression both physically and emotionally, they become stored inside the body. Many individuals report feeling a sense of relief when they begin to give a voice to these stored emotions. The physical relief you may feel as you put your feelings into words is evidence that the emotions are running their course and doing what they were designed to do.

CHAPTER 6

Turning to Her Instead

There's more to recovering from an addiction than identifying our emotions. Once we get better at acknowledging when we're feeling bad, what do we do with those feelings? Feelings arise as a way of telling us that there's something we need. To successfully move beyond an ingrained porn habit, we must develop other, better ways of trying to meet our needs.

Uncomfortable emotions can show up without warning, much like a pebble in the shoe often shows up out of nowhere. I tell my clients that using pornography to numb out difficult emotions is like taking morphine to deal with a pebble in your shoe. Of course, it seems silly to numb out the whole body in order to deal with something as simple as a pebble in a shoe.

Pain, whether emotional or physical, is designed to direct our attention to something that needs to be addressed. The pain of the pebble in the shoe directs our attention to the foot for an immediate solution. Although emotional pain may not be that simple to resolve, the pain still directs our attention so we can do something about it. This is a great chance to use the soul's natural mechanism for self-correction instead of simply numbing out the distressing emotions. Both the pebble and emotional pain require us to slow down, notice, locate the source of pain, and then listen inwardly in order to understand what we really need.

What We Really Need When We Go to Porn

The U.S. Food and Drug Administration gives us dietary guidance by way of its Recommended Daily Allowance (RDA). Scientists have done extensive research to determine which nutrients we need to maintain our physical health and how much of each we should be taking in.

If there were a similar index for our souls, what would be on it? What would the Recommended Daily Allowance of porn be? Our souls need about the same amount of porn as our bodies need of carcinogens. But if that would not be on the list, what would be there instead?

What we actually *need* is pretty basic, although it's easy to miss our daily dose. We need human connection. In the movie *Cast Away,* Tom Hanks plays Chuck Noland, a business executive stranded on a tropical island after his cargo plane crash-lands in the ocean. Chuck discovers a volleyball in some packages that wash ashore his deserted island. In a subsequent fit of frustration with his circumstances, Chuck picks up the volleyball and throws it into the ocean. This interaction begins a long relationship with the volleyball, which Chuck names "Wilson."

Chuck's connection to Wilson causes him to talk to the ball, carry it around the island, and even protect the ball from being hurt. In the final heartbreaking scene of his castaway experience, Chuck loses track of Wilson as the ball floats out into the ocean away from the crudely constructed escape raft. Panicked, he reflexively jumps into the ocean to rescue Wilson. Tired, out of breath, and nearly drowning, Chuck gives up and cries out to Wilson that he's sorry he can't rescue him.

This moving scene would seem silly without understanding the relationship Chuck had formed with Wilson over his five years of isolation on the island. He needed Wilson and believed Wilson needed him.

No one watching this movie needs to have this explained. Everyone seems to accept naturally that seeking connection is as important to Chuck as fire, food, shelter, and water.

Reaching when we're in need is something our nervous systems are hardwired to prompt us to do. It happens automatically, instinctively, and it helps us survive. The first few seconds of life outside the womb involve a baby crying and reaching for comfort. No one told the baby that those behaviors would help, and no one has to tell the mother and father how to respond. Instinctively, they do what they can to soothe and comfort the distressed infant.

We also knew as toddlers what we needed when we felt emotionally raw or needy, insecure, or unsure of ourselves. We were natural experts, sensing instinctively how to handle such times. We looked to Mom or Dad in hopes that they'd listen, really see that we were struggling, and empathize. That's what hit the spot in a deep-down, soul-satisfying way. We knew we needed their support.

Not only did we know at a very young age that we needed closeness and connection, we knew instinctively how to get it. We hadn't yet learned to pretend, hide, camouflage, or beat around the bush as we too often do as adults. We went directly for it. Picture a toddler who, seeing Mom and Dad hugging and feeling left out, wedges himself in between them. It's just as potent, though less overt, in a teenager lingering in the kitchen after she gets home at night, waiting for someone to ask about her day.

There is a satisfaction that comes from feeling close to and being understood by our number-one attachment figure. And that's not just for kids. Remember psychiatrist John Bowlby's assertion: This need for emotional connection and relationship support extends from the cradle to the grave. Every one of us, at every age, has an ongoing need to reach out, confident that we'll find someone who is there for us when we're in need.

Emotional ups and downs are a regular part of our lives. We are in need a lot of the time. We need to know that when we're in need, that special someone will be there for us. Each time he or she responds to our call for comfort, the person becomes ever more important to us. The experience has strengthened the attachment between us. The lid was off the superglue when we were feeling raw, and so now we're more bonded than ever.

Geoff and our colleague Rebecca Jorgensen have coined the term "co-regulation" to describe this relationship dynamic of reaching for and providing physical and emotional comfort to one another. The same way we get more of what we need by joining a co-op, we get more of what we need when we co-regulate. Babies and small children cannot self-regulate. Even though we have more ability to self-regulate as we get older, it's more powerful and effective to depend on one another, to co-regulate when we need help feeling soothed and comforted.

Co-regulation may seem like an immature or regressive thing to do, especially since we actually possess the ability as adults to self-regulate. But all we need to do to be reminded of how powerful our need is to co-regulate is to attend a funeral. Widows or widowers have just lost their primary attachment figures, and they are often surrounded by the hugs, touch, closeness, and connection of those around them. This is a temporary substitute to help the bereaved cope with the loss. We don't expect them to self-regulate during such times. Even though we become less dependent on others to care for our physical needs, we have a lifelong need to know someone is there for us and cares about how we feel.

Unfortunately, over the years we may have learned to stop doing what once came naturally. For various reasons, we may have concluded that it wasn't such a great idea. It hasn't gone well for us. Perhaps we have suffered disappointment or deprivation at key times when we reached out. Or maybe we feel ashamed of the needs that would otherwise prompt the urge to reach out. We're loath to look weak, thin-skinned, wimpy, unmanly. Instead of reaching out for support when we're emotionally distressed, we keep our feelings inside. We try to stuff our feelings back down when they threaten to bubble up to the surface. We pretend that what hurts us emotionally or unsettles our world a bit really doesn't. We may become so good at pretending we're not upset by upsetting stuff that we convince ourselves to not reach out and open up.

However, emotions that have been buried alive don't just die off. All of their potency and energy remains primed and ready to drive us—if not in the direction of expressing ourselves in a way that enables those emotions to discharge as they're shared, then in the direction of our most self-defeating habit. The feelings that prime us to seek emotional connection and relationship support can also prime us to relapse to our addiction.

Since going to an addictive substance such as pornography can activate some of the same chemical processes that are involved when we make an emotional connection with a real person, a certain level of temporary relief does come. But we also become less able to get what we need from relationships. Craig Nakken, author of *The Addictive Personality,* has stated that "the longer an addictive illness progresses, the less a person feels the ability to have meaningful relationships with others. Addiction makes life very lonely and isolated, which creates more of a need for the addict to act out. When the addict hurts, he or she will act out by turning to the addiction for relief, just as someone else may turn to a spouse, a best friend, or spiritual beliefs. For the addict, the mood change created by acting out gives the illusion that a need has been met" (Nakken 1996, 11). This illusion of connection offers such quick relief that the idea of working to have a lasting connection with another person may feel laborious and unpredictable.

When an individual is going to pornography, it's actually a "reaching out" motion, seeking the same kind of comfort and connection that a healthy relationship with an attachment figure can provide. In a healthy attachment bond, the distressed individual knows the other is going to reach back when he or she reaches for comfort and connection. If there are times when the connection breaks down, then both partners know that they can come back together and try again later until the secure bond is reestablished. Pornography mimics this same responsiveness and accessibility. As a counterfeit attachment, pornography consistently soothes and relieves the distress of the person who is relying on it. That pseudo-regulation of the emotions and body is part of the draw of pornography.

Those who've become hooked on porn discovered at some point that reaching out to pornography is a reliable attachment— even more so than another human being. Even though humans can be accessible, responsive, comforting, and soothing, pornography is much more predictable and ever available to offer relief. Porn demands no vulnerability or emotional risk. When you reach to pornography, you know it will be there for you. So, when your wife feels that she has to compete with the physical attractiveness of women depicted in pornography, in reality, what she's up against is the emotional dynamic of the instant relief and comfort you can receive when you turn to the pornography instead of to her. However, she can rest assured that pornography has *nothing* on her ability to provide deep, lasting, and true emotional relief and comfort. Pornography can never ultimately satisfy like true attachment.

A pornography-dependent individual is always reaching for something. If he pulls away from his partner and seeks out porn, he's reaching for the comfort of porn. If he shuts out his partner emotionally and doesn't share what's on his mind, he's reaching inside for comfort and relief instead of reaching out to others. In recovery, it's important to keep noticing where the reaching is directed. Is the person learning to reach out to a group, to a church leader, to a spouse, to a parent, to a friend, to a therapist, to God? Is the recovering addict working to nurture that inborn reflex to reach out instead of in? Is the person working to create and repair connections that will help him or her continue to reach out for real connection instead of acting out with pornography?

Turning to Her for Help in Your Struggle against Porn

I remember trying to convince one client, Ivan, when we began working together, that he should disclose to his wife that he had recently been struggling with pornography again. "I don't think I can bring myself to tell her," he insisted. "Four different times now she's become aware of my struggle, and each time it's been so hard on our marriage. Last time she admitted that she would have left me by now if it weren't for how hard it would be on the children. I'm afraid that if she becomes aware that I'm struggling again, it will end up being the final straw."

Ivan was hoping that through his work with me he would overcome this problem once and for all. "Then I'll clean everything up with her and at church," he said. "The problem is that I have confessed so many times to different ecclesiastical leaders and to my wife, but those confessions have never changed things. I don't want to go through all that again right now until I know that this time will be different."

"Well," I responded, "besides coming in to see me, at this point 'this time' doesn't look very different at all from past times. You say that you have confessed so many times, but haven't you always kept this problem a secret and only told your wife about the nature and extent of the problem once she discovered evidence of it or caught you in the act?"

Ivan acknowledged that this was the way things had always gone. At my suggestion, Ivan decided to talk to his wife, Tina, and set up a plan with her to approach the problem in a completely different way, with a completely new set of ground rules. He made a commitment to be honest with her and to tell her immediately, within an hour at the most, of any pornography viewing. He took her for a drive on a Sunday evening while the kids were with Grandma and Grandpa.

"Honey, you know that this has been an on-and-off struggle for a long time," he told her. "I've become convinced that I can no longer continue vacillating between being completely free from it at times and being totally under pornography's control at other times if I hope to preserve our marriage. To avoid those times when I struggle so deeply and over an extended period of time, I need to let you in on what's happening earlier on, at those times when I'm just starting to get caught up in it again. Then you can see the process in its earliest stages and help me during those times. Those are the times I usually keep it a secret because I'm so ashamed. Of course, it's easier to keep it a secret then because the evidence is just starting to accrue. In the past, I've wanted to keep you from being hurt and angry, so I struggle on my own. Of course, I also manage to rationalize that I'm not yet in very deep. I tell myself, 'It was just once. I'll steer clear of it again from now on and that one time doesn't have to be a big deal.' Of course, that just sets the stage for me to later think, 'I've already given in once. What's one more time?' I never plan on getting back in over my head, but that's inevitably what happens. Then I think, 'I can't tell her now; she'll be mad that I've kept this much a secret!'

"With all of the struggles I've had—having engaged in hundreds of pornography-viewing sessions—my best guess now is that I'll probably succumb to temptation again, maybe even several times, before I'll be able to give it up for good. Therefore, I want to ask for your help in containing my future lapses before they get out of hand. I wish I could commit to 'never touching the stuff again' with some confidence that I'll follow through. However, you've seen how well it goes when I do that. But I know I can make and stick with the following commitment: If I do give in to temptation, I will never let more than an hour elapse before I contact you and let you know what I've done. It will be hard for me, but if I know that we're going to work together to conquer this problem, that will give me the strength to do it."

Tina was indeed angry and hurt when he disclosed that he had gone back to this old habit that had so damaged their relationship. However, it didn't end up being the "final straw" for her. She was willing, albeit skeptical at first, to go along with the approach he was suggesting.

Ivan was alone in a hotel room the first time he viewed pornography after making that commitment. He was embarrassed to call and wake up Tina at 1:15 in the morning. He almost talked himself into putting it off until the next morning. "Couldn't I do it during the first *waking* hour after a slip?" he asked himself. He was also afraid to tell her over the phone. He almost rationalized to himself that he could tell her "within an hour of seeing her in person." However, he decided to stay true to the commitment he had made.

Tina recalled, "I was groggy when I answered the phone, but I immediately came fully to my senses when I heard Ivan's voice on the phone and realized what he was calling about. I was so angry, maybe it was a good thing he wasn't there. Here I was taking care of the kids, working harder than ever because he was away on a business trip, and he was entertaining himself in a way that took him even further from me and the family. I was so upset. I let him have it over the phone."

"That was hard for me," Ivan recalled, "but you'd have to understand the hell I've put myself through in the past to understand it when I say that it was actually a relief to have it out in the open. If I hadn't called and told her, I would have been slinking around the next morning trying to focus on my work commitments with a lump in my throat and a dark cloud over me. Then I'd have been tempted to get another fix of pornography to numb the guilt and shame I was feeling. This time, I felt stronger for having faced up to my wife about what I had done. I didn't argue with anything she said. I accepted it as the consequences of my actions.

"That, perhaps, is the biggest difference this policy of immediate honesty has made for me," Ivan concluded. "Before, I could get caught up in enjoying the engine of the train—viewing the pornography—and then delude myself into thinking that it might not have a caboose—the effect the pornography viewing had on my wife. I tried to take the pleasure without facing the pain. Of course, as soon as the engine passes, you know for sure that the caboose is on its way. So I would try my best to outrun it, thinking, 'If I can just work hard enough to do better, be careful enough not to let my secret out, no one ever has to know.' What I was really hoping was that I would never have to suffer for my choices. Of course, it never worked out that way. Well, having suffered in that way over so many years, it was refreshing to stand up and face the caboose. I felt like I was regaining my integrity—not completely yet, because I had violated her trust in me and my own values by viewing pornography, but it felt like I was getting back on track."

Initially, Tina was afraid that she might not be able to bear hearing about all of Ivan's struggles along the way. "The entire problem is so repulsive and horrible to me. I assumed that a yucky feeling would linger with me all the time once I knew he had succumbed. Fortunately, it was easier than I thought it would be to say, 'I'm sorry you made that choice, Ivan,' and then in my mind add, 'I'm glad it's your problem to solve, not mine.'"

Ivan viewed pornography a handful of times over the subsequent year and a half. Now, three years since his last struggle, Tina recalls some of the benefits of Ivan's commitment to immediate honesty:

"I had told Ivan many times, so I'm not sure why it took him so long to finally get it, that his lying was always a bigger threat to our marriage than the pornography. The viewing of pornography took up less than 1 percent of his time. He might make the decision to do that on an impulse. On the other hand, following that act, he had to deceive me 100 percent of the time to keep it a secret. He was being dishonest every hour of the day, every day of the week, sometimes for months on end. After the first two or three slips he had, I really came to trust that he would tell me within minutes of having a problem. Then I stopped worrying. I didn't have to wonder—when we were on a date, when we were in bed together as a couple, when we were sitting in church, when he was playing with the kids—how well he was dealing with this problem. I finally knew all the time *exactly* how he was doing, for a change. I didn't have to try to read his mind or be a detective. I stopped wondering and feeling like I had to ask him about it all the time."

TURNING TO HER FURTHER UPSTREAM

When we suggest to our clients who struggle with pornography that they will benefit greatly in their recovery by opening up to their partners, most of them assume we want them to discuss only their relapses and struggles. Although it's important for a wife to know how well her husband is managing his struggles with pornography, those conversations alone won't repair the broken connection experienced by the couple.

Some men are reluctant to open up to their wives about any of their triggers, fearing that it will make things worse for both of them. Due to the potential pain created with such a confusing dilemma, most men eventually pull away from their wives and seek out support from others to do this work. They just don't know how to talk about their struggles. As a result, a wife may only hear from her husband about his emotional struggles when he approaches her to disclose a relapse. Of course, by that time, she may not believe there is much she can do. She may feel stuck, wondering how best to respond to his efforts to open up to her.

Husband and wife can help each other if he recognizes and shares the deeper emotions that drive the cravings for relief. This will help her see that he's coming to her long before the emotions become sexualized in the form of seeking relief through pornography. If he connects to those emotional undercurrents and brings those to her early in the process, she's going to have an easier time knowing how to respond to him. In fact, both of them will be less overwhelmed by these emotions, as he won't be as afraid of relapsing and feeling completely ashamed of himself, and she won't experience what he's sharing with her as a betrayal.

He may not know how to ask her for what he needs from her (which is what activated the whole cycle in the first place), but his efforts to come to her earlier in the process will help him connect to those important emotions that will protect both him and his relationship.

Most women we work with tell us they want to know how to respond in a helpful way, but most of what gets brought to them is so disconnected from their husbands' real emotions that they aren't sure how to respond. Although a wife might be able to understand there might be feelings underneath her husband's sexual triggers, his efforts to identify and bring them to her earlier will help both of them.

Partners can learn to be there for each other when he works to understand the currents that are building below the surface and she works to hear what he's trying to say to her. This keeps them from going through the rapids of disconnection and over the waterfall of relapse.

In the Sexaholics Anonymous twelve-step group meetings he had started attending, Ben heard other attendees talk about the importance of "rigorous honesty." He remembered how distraught Kristy had been when she talked about feeling he had violated her trust. He knew that secrecy had contributed not only to her mistrust but also to the persistence of his problem. Ben resolved to be completely honest with Kristy about his struggles and feelings from then on.

Now that the problem was out in the open and he and Kristy were working together on it, Ben experienced fewer cravings than he had before. As time wore on, however, the old urges to view pornography started to hit him again. On tough days, he would let Kristy know about them. Although she appreciated his openness, she was concerned that he was still struggling.

During one counseling session, it was apparent there was unresolved tension between them. "I told her I was struggling," Ben said. "She asked for more information. I wasn't sure whether or not I should tell her. I knew it might hurt her if I told the truth."

In an effort to be rigorously honest, he had told her that, while driving around in his van for work that afternoon, he had stopped at a traffic light. A black convertible had pulled up next to him with an attractive woman at the wheel. "I hate to admit it, but she caught my attention and I started to fantasize. I told Kristy about it. She was upset. Then she wanted to know more about the woman, what she looked like and what about her I found attractive. She wanted to know all about the fantasy, but it was just a brief lapse; my mind was just beginning to wander. The fantasy hadn't developed into anything very detailed. I don't really even remember all that much about the woman. But Kristy assumed I wouldn't tell her more because I knew it would upset her even more. She thought I was holding back. I tried to think back and see if any other thoughts had come into my mind. But then my mind was on that topic again, thinking sexual thoughts about a strange woman. I told Kristy that I didn't think it was good for us to dwell on it."

"*He* told *me* it wasn't a good idea for him to dwell it," Kristy said. "Of course it isn't. That's exactly why I'm so frustrated with him. Why does he keep doing it?"

Many things can trigger unwanted sexual thoughts in someone who has a history of sexually acting out. Stress, feelings of isolation, visual cues, and even boredom are common triggers. Sexual thoughts are like a lightning rod. They can draw all of our energy and attention. They are a powerful symptom of an inner struggle. However, when we dwell on the symptom, we can miss the cause and, more important, the cure. Being forthcoming about having sexual thoughts is one part of honesty, but it's not the biggest part, nor is it the most important.

We encourage clients like Ben to pay attention inwardly, to be on the lookout for other feelings and needs that might be in play when sexual urges hit. If he feels lonely because he's out driving on his own all day, it might be a relief to think about sex instead. However, those sexual thoughts are obscuring something much more important. He needs to be honest with himself, rigorously honest, by acknowledging the loneliness. The sexual thoughts are closer to the surface. It's easier—and may seem manlier—to feel sexually interested or aroused. It's more difficult to admit more vulnerable feelings and softer inner experiences. He needs to start by being honest with himself about what he's feeling before he can be deeply honest with his wife.

The next time Ben told Kristy he had been tempted that day, she saw the usual bait, but she didn't take it. Instead of asking about the content of his tempting thoughts, she was more interested in what, in particular, had happened that day to make him vulnerable.

"What had your day been like up to that point?" she asked.

"Kind of a drag, I guess," Ben responded.

"What was going on inside for you?" Kristy asked.

Ben pondered her question and thought back. He couldn't put his finger on anything. Still, that brief discussion helped him to feel hopeful and cared about and to be on the lookout the next time temptation hit. He was in a more curious frame of mind a few days later when illicit thoughts kept popping into his mind.

"Sex is the most attention-grabbing feeling, but what else is going on for me?" he wondered. "I'm driving around replacing copier toner cartridges, and it's boring. I know that's part of it. It's hard to see people driving around in nice cars. I go into offices with all of these sharp professionals. Am I envious? Seems like they have important things to do and places to be. Do I feel less important than them? Sometimes I wish I'd been pickier and more deliberate about my career path. I don't feel like I'm living up to my potential."

Ben's face was getting warm and there was a lump in his throat. "Sometimes I suspect that other people are looking down on me. I guess that's why it's nice when women find me attractive. It makes me feel like I still have it. Like I'm worth paying attention to. That I'm admired and important, like I have something to offer."

Ben knew immediately that it would be much tougher to be honest with Kristy about these feelings. After the kids were in bed that night, he talked to her about what he had felt that afternoon. As he did, the feelings came back.

Sitting on the side of the bed, he looked down at the floor as he shared his self-doubts. "Part of it is that you were with your old boyfriend for three and a half years before we got together. His roofing business is thriving now." Ben's throat almost wouldn't let the next words out: "Do you ever regret marrying me, with all the financial struggles we've had?"

Kristy looked Ben in the eye. "The financial struggles have been the easiest part," she said. They both laughed. It felt good to both of them to laugh together, with how painful things had been. "None of our struggles have ever made me sorry I chose you. I watch you in the backyard kicking the ball with Trevor. I see you wrestling with Isaac. Little Crystal just can't help herself from jumping into the melee. I'd never trade you in and take a chance on my kids having a different father." Kristy thought for a few moments. "Even the hard stuff, we've done it all *together.* We're spending our Saturday afternoons fixing the flood damage in the basement because we can't afford to hire it out—listening while we work to the oldies station and CDs no one else would like but us. The funny thing is, that time together is precious to me. It's just the two of us working. I wouldn't have it any other way. I cherish all my memories of times like that with you." Ben felt as if she was looking straight into his soul now. "I love *you,* Ben. I love that you're willing to work so hard doing stuff you don't really like to support our family. I don't want any other man. I want you. Which is why it hurts when I'm afraid that you don't desire me. When I worry about your attractions to other women or sense you're hiding something, I feel so unsure. I want so badly to know I can trust you and feel secure in your love."

"Look what I've done to you," Ben said. Looking into his eyes, Kristy knew that he had really heard her, was genuinely seeing how much she had been hurting. "I don't want to minimize my sexual problems," Ben said, "because I know they've fueled your insecurity. But I do want you to know that my struggles are my struggles; they have nothing to do with your attractiveness or desirability. Everything I've done so far in my recovery, and everything I'll do in the future, I'm doing because I want to be—I want to become—the kind of man that you can count on, that you can put all your trust in. That is who I want to be. I know these are just words, but I'm going to keep doing whatever I need to do for the rest of my life to show you that I mean what I'm saying."

These types of heart-to-heart discussions continued to happen with Ben and Kristy. They not only helped their relationship recover but they helped Ben overcome his old pattern. It takes a while for most couples to learn to communicate about their deeper feelings and ask for their needs to be met the way Kristy and Ben did. Each partner's history and insecurities can create an entire minefield of other less helpful reactions that can be set off along the way. As couples keep trying, however, the understanding they develop can change everything. Each is more likely to see the other's deepest, once-obscured needs and become more able to help meet them. As understanding and communication deepen, distress lessens and tensions diffuse. A wife finds it easier to relate to and identify with a husband when he talks about the quieter, more genuine aspects of what's going on inside him. This is the same man whose sexual struggles may have only weeks ago put her off so much that she wondered, "What kind of man did I marry?"

This is the powerful nature of the crisis in marriage that pornography can ignite. It can tear couples apart. Or, if both partners are willing, the struggle can be used as an opportunity to draw together, becoming stronger and more united.

The Courage to Be Real

It can be extremely difficult to stay with what we're feeling, and even more challenging to convey it to another person, when we feel emotionally raw. It is a time when many people, particularly men, are more prone to pull back from other people and stay inside themselves. Men not only have more difficulty than women making eye contact with others, they are also socialized to avoid anything that appears feminine.

In one study (Wexler 2009), three groups of men were instructed to keep their hands in a tub of icy water as long as they possibly could. One group of men was told that the ability to endure the discomfort of the cold water was a measure of male sex hormones, performance, and physical fitness. A second group was told it was a measure of female sex hormones, and a third group was told nothing. As expected, the first group kept their hands in ice-cold water the longest. The study showed how much physical pain a man is willing to endure if his manhood is under scrutiny.

Most men are socialized to focus on performance and discouraged from relying on other people for support. Feelings and situations that may make them appear weak or vulnerable are difficult for most men. It's hard enough to be vulnerable. It's especially hard to reach out to the one person who is most important to a man, even though she's the one with whom he ought to feel the safest.

Such was the case for Glen, who said during our first session, "I've never been a good communicator. I keep things inside." He recalled not wanting to be a bother to other people from quite a young age. His parents had divorced when he was six, and he remembered thinking that his mom had enough on her plate just dealing with her work at the post office, feeding the family, and paying the bills. Plus, his sister had a learning disability and required quite a bit of help with homework. Although Glen recalled feeling lonely at times, he made the best of the situation by riding his bike around and exploring the foothills near their home. He said, "I had a dog I could talk to—Lucy. And I actually did talk to old Luce, quite a bit."

Glen's wife, Melanie, accompanied him to the next session. She said at one point, "I'm open with Glen about everything. He knows when I'm not happy about something. With him it's a different story. Sometimes I can see that something's eating at him when he's upset, but he won't say anything. He doesn't come and talk to me about it. Maybe it's because I have a bad temper and he's afraid he'll set me off."

Glen acknowledged that that was exactly what went on inside for him. "I don't want to hurt anybody. I don't want to approach her with anything that would upset her or make her feel bad. I don't even approach her for sex, and it bothers her that I don't."

"Sometimes I wish he'd be more aggressive," Melanie chimed in. "I've told him, 'Just come and take me sometime. Pursue me.' It would be so nice if he'd put himself out there with me and let me know, in no uncertain terms, what he was feeling or what he wanted."

When I proposed that there were usually emotional precursors to addictive behavior, Glen wasn't so sure that applied in his case. However, he was willing to entertain the possibility. He also committed to experiment by opening up to Melanie about what went on inside for him, even though he knew it would be very challenging.

It didn't take long before he had something to open up about. One month into our work together, Glen admitted that he was getting frustrated about how things were going at home. They had learned that Melanie was pregnant, and she was much more tired than usual. She spent a lot of her time lying down, resting, and playing on the computer. The previous night Glen had arrived home at seven o'clock to a couple of days' worth of dishes piled in the sink and toys strewn on the floor throughout the house. He had his son and daughter help straighten up the messes they had made and then started attacking the dishes. As he was finishing up at the sink, Melanie said, "Maybe we'd better pull some chicken out of the freezer." Glen looked up at the clock: 8:00 p.m.

In my office Glen was shaking his head as he thought about that night. "I was trying to be Superdad and Superhusband for a week; now I'm starting to dip into my ornery phase. I work late and come home to more work. I don't wind down before I go to bed so I end up feeling too tense to fall asleep. Or I take time to wind down and then I'm up late watching TV or on the computer and I don't get enough sleep." I asked Glen if he'd gotten back into a pattern of viewing pornography. He looked at me sheepishly and was hesitant at first, but then acknowledged that he'd viewed it a couple of times over the last few days.

I started to explore with Glen what had been going on for him emotionally during this difficult time. "What goes on inside for you when you walk in and she's at the computer and there's lots of work to do?"

"First, I tell myself that she's pregnant with my child. She's doing this amazing, physically brutal thing. She's making this sacrifice for our family, for us. I need to suck it up. That helps me get to work on what needs doing, even though I've just put in a twelve-hour day at work. *However* . . . over time I start to feel bad. I get resentful. Last night I looked over at her, distracted at the computer, and thought, *I am not important to her. The thought of me and what I need hasn't even registered to her. It feels like I'm on my own. I don't have a partner here.*"

As we explored what had gone on the previous Saturday, the night he had first used pornography again after a month and a half of abstaining, we discovered that a lot of the same feelings had been stirred up. "She seemed checked-out physically, but also emotionally as she sat at the computer. She was tired and ready for bed early, but I wanted to stay up. If she'd had more energy to stay up and be with me, I would have felt more like we were a couple. I'd been feeling lonely, even at those times when she had asked me to lie there and hold her. It doesn't feel like our relationship right now. It feels like she's a shell of herself."

I reminded Glen about how vulnerable feelings take the lid off our emotional superglue: When we feel most in need, we are most primed to become dependent. He is in need but feels like he can't talk to Melanie about how he's feeling. If he could, that might bring relief. He needs some bridge out of distress. If that bridge—communication in his marriage—is not open for traffic, he's going to be a lot more tempted to take the old faithful one—pornography.

I challenged him to open up to Melanie about how he was feeling—not to blame her, but just to share his struggles. "Let her off the hook. Tell her she doesn't need to change a thing. But you need to share. You can't afford to keep this stuff in."

The following week Glen described how challenging it had been to start the conversation when he was feeling frustrated and unimportant. "It was tough. The first couple of nights I couldn't get around to talking to her about how I was feeling. Tuesday night I worked late. Got home at 6:15 to find the usual mess and no dinner in sight. I had a meeting with the Boy Scout troop that I help lead at 7:00 that night. I said, 'This frustrates me. I've been working hard and you're on the computer. I'm not going to get dinner.' She seemed to take it okay. I let her know, 'Just because I'm saying this to you doesn't mean you have to make it better or change what you're doing. I'm just learning that I can't afford to hold this in.' Monday night I'd just done my usual, trying to pick up the slack without saying anything. I'd felt tense all night. But Tuesday night was a contrast. I felt really good after that communication. I went to Scouts. Ate cold tacos when I got home at about 8:30; I didn't like that. But I felt calmer; there was a different mood. It wasn't like there was a pillar of light or the voice of angels or anything, but it was better."

Throughout the coming weeks, Melanie continued to feel quite taxed by her pregnancy. It was hard for Glen. Two weeks later he said, "She doesn't want to do much besides taking baths and showers. I went trick-or-treating alone with the kids. It feels like it gets heavier and heavier over time to carry the burden. But I've noticed that once I open up to her, it seems to help reset things. The burden gets off-loaded, for some reason, even though she's not able to do any more than before. The fact that she'll listen to what I'm feeling and seems to care makes a big difference. It's like we're partners at heart, even if I can't be pregnant for her and she can't take on more of the burdens of family life."

Glen also reported that over time he was becoming less afraid of conflict. "I talked to her last Tuesday night and said, 'I have Scouts every week. We really need a different plan for dinner on Tuesday night.' She argued back at me. I said, 'Whoa, I'm just trying to communicate!' She said, 'I'm communicating back! Arguing is communicating!' When it was all said and done, I wasn't sorry I had brought it up, and I don't think she felt blamed, either. It felt good not to hold it in, even though we had a bit of a conflict over it."

I asked Glen how intense the temptations to seek pornography had been lately.

"I've had a crappy week at work, and I can tell that I would really be feeling on edge by now if I had let the stress build up. If I weren't conveying more of my true feelings at home, I think it would be overwhelming. Instead, the stress feels more manageable now. Likewise, if I catch myself having a sexual urge or craving, I'm diverting myself more easily. And I do think there's a connection: When I'm more stressed and holding it in, I'm tempted to go to that for comfort. When I unload my stress by talking about what I'm feeling, I get the relief more directly, in a better way."

A week or so later, Glen reported, "Some of the usual issues came up this week—stress at work, stress at home, but as Melanie and I are closer they didn't affect me as much as usual."

Glen's statement reminded me of a growing body of research demonstrating that relationships can provide a very powerful buffering between us and the stresses that would otherwise impact us. In one such study, female subjects were asked to hold a hand submerged in cold water for as long as they could stand it. This is a pretty straightforward measure of how much stress people can tolerate: a longer length of time in the water equates to a greater capacity for tolerating stress. Some of the women looked at a photograph of their romantic partner as they held their hands under the water, while others didn't. Those who had that simple reminder of their primary support system lasted significantly longer in the ice water than those who didn't (Master et al. 2009). *Emotional connection and relationship support do provide what we really need when we're stressed.* Pornography is a lousy counterfeit. It dissipates some of the emotion temporarily but leaves us worse off in the long run.

Many a woman in Melanie's shoes will report later that even though her husband was really good at keeping his pornography consumption a secret, she had always felt that there was something he had been holding back. Despite years of marriage, he remained, to her, a somewhat mysterious character.

Once men start opening up the way Glen did, their wives often report feeling tremendous relief, a sense that they are finally beginning to truly get to know their husbands. A wife in this situation feels a growing confidence that he is being real with her—and perhaps even with himself—for the first time. When he comes home to his emotions, he feels an increased sense of comfort about being in his own skin. This growing sense of openness on his part also leaves his wife feeling more confident in his recovery from addiction. She is less apt to check the history on his Internet browser or grill him about how he spends his free time. Once she has her finger on his emotional pulse in this way, she has the sense that she really knows what's up with him. She doesn't have to wonder and search and guess and cross-examine, none of which ever left her feeling truly, deeply at peace anyway.

IT TAKES BRUTE COURAGE TO OWN OUR NEEDINESS

Trappist monk and Catholic writer Thomas Merton said, "Sometimes the invitation to beauty may come to us masked as humiliating sickness or weakness." This lesson was driven home to me as I worked with Leon, a client who came from out of town to receive intensive treatment at our clinic and also a fellow mental health professional who works with child abuse victims and their families. He came to see us because he had been trying to rely on an addiction to bring a spark of excitement and renewed motivation to a life that had been drained of its passion by a decade and a half of overwhelming professional demands. Although he came in seeking help with his addiction, we quickly discovered that his habit was not only a problem, it was a solution. Of course, it was a bad solution that had created even more problems in his life, but it was at least an attempt to stem the burnout he was suffering as a professional.

As Leon was nearing the end of his treatment, we talked together about a deep shift that had taken place in his perspective: "I've always seen myself as someone who needs to be strong enough to help others. This theme even showed up in my taste for literature. I must have read the first hundred pages of *Les Misérables* half a dozen times over the years. I was so inspired by the story. I love the priest's generosity and grace. He reached into lives and gave exactly what was needed. He gave up his church

147

and allowed the building to be used as a hospital. And, of course, there was what he did for Valjean: When the poor man had really made a mess of things and had no way out on his own, the priest stepped in. He forgave him without even being asked. Even though he had been robbed of his silver, he stepped in and gave even more—the candlesticks and complete forgiveness. He spared the man the consequences of his own actions. He offered grace to one who had not even thought to seek it.

"What I have learned in the process of trying to recover from my addiction," Leon continued, "is that in the story of my life, my role is not that of the priest, as I always wanted it to be. I realize now that I am Valjean! I am continually drawn back to that story because I crave the kind of grace he received. I want to be cared for and spared suffering. For years, I felt like my role was just to provide that for others. As hard as I tried, however, it seemed that I just didn't have it in me. I felt like a charlatan. Now I'm finally beginning to see that I don't need to be ashamed of my weakness. I don't have to be the source of that goodness, I can be the recipient. I can let others help me. I can rely on the grace of God. I can receive support from loved ones. I don't need to be the one who only gives. In fact, I can't. I'm not the vine; I'm only a branch, if anything. It's okay for me to be in Valjean's shoes."

As Leon talked, I realized that he even looked physically lighter than he had when he had first arrived at our clinic. "This wisdom and freedom," he said, "I owe to my addiction. It was the only weakness blatant enough that I could no longer keep pretending that it wasn't there. I was so proud of my role as the strong one, the help*er,* that I don't think I ever would have willingly acknowledged my own neediness and put myself in the role of recipient. I would have almost preferred death to the shame and humiliation of having my addiction discovered. But it forced me into the position of being the needy one for a change, and for that I will be forever grateful."

Ralph Waldo Emerson said, "There is a crack in everything God has made." In our pride, we want to deny that we have any cracks. We cram putty in them and walk around pretending we're fine. However, it is only by way of accepting our needs that we can open up the possibility of their being met. In the words of Polish philosopher Leszek Kolakowski, "The Sacred is revealed to us in the experience of our failure . . . the awareness of human insufficiency . . . the lived admission of failure."

ACCEPTING AND CONVEYING OUR NEEDINESS

It's no wonder it took a while for another client, Earl, to see the connection between feeling bad and being tempted to act out sexually. It was often a day or more after something hurt his feelings before he would become prone to escape by fantasizing about sex. Even after he did trace his way back to emotionally charged events, Earl was reluctant at first to talk about them because he felt like they were silly little things and he was embarrassed that he'd had such a strong reaction to them. Seeing some of his coworkers pull into the parking lot after they'd gone out to lunch together without inviting him, for instance. He had brought his lunch from home, he reasoned, so that wasn't anything to feel bad over. Even when he tried to dismiss and disown those kinds of emotional reactions, however, he became more aware as we worked together that his mood sometimes took a distinctly darker turn when events like that occurred in his life. They left him feeling more down, and then the resulting down state became fertile ground in which addictive cravings could take root, sprout, and grow.

Earl learned how helpful it was to talk such feelings out. One day he told me about his most recent close call. It had been three in the afternoon, and he'd long ago observed that he was more at risk in the afternoon at work. He'd gotten on the Internet to take a much-needed break from spreadsheets and customer calls. However, checking the usual news sites, sports scores, and extended family blog had left him still unsatisfied and feeling more than the usual reluctance to return to the grindstone. "I was that close to going back to my old standby," he recalled.

Earl couldn't identify anything earlier that day that had made him feel bad or might have put him at risk in some other way. "What about yesterday?" I asked.

"Yesterday was my birthday," he said. "There was no shortage of things to feel good about. My wife threw a little family party for me and everyone sang 'Happy Birthday.'" He sat quietly for a minute as he thought back on the evening. "You know, I feel ungrateful and kind of wimpy for saying this because Carolyn went to a lot of trouble to think about me . . . and make spice cake, my favorite . . . but whenever we get together with my in-laws, it does quickly become a walk down memory lane for the Russell clan. It's easy to feel left out. I guess I need to own that more: I do get feeling left out. Yeah," Earl said with a sigh, "that's what it was. I've always had a thing about birthdays being a special day. All about that person. You know, as kids we were let off the hook for all our usual chores on our birthdays. I'd like to have felt more like it was about me on my birthday." Earl was quiet now, introspective. Then, breaking his reverie, he looked at me sheepishly. "Is that totally immature and selfish?"

"I have a different question for you," I responded. "Was it real?"

"Yeah," he said with a shrug and a smile. "I guess it was."

I might be attaching too much significance to that particular moment, but it always seems to me at such times that I'm watching people come home to themselves—to their real selves, warts and all, not just who they wish they were or are trying to be—and settling in. It's a nice, satisfying thing to see.

How our spouses respond when we get real can be very important. After Earl left my office that day, I thought about all the unhelpful ways I might respond if I were in his wife's shoes and he told me that he felt bad on his birthday. "Birthday wasn't good enough for you, huh? Do you know I went to the grocery store twice that day—first to get eggs and then later because we didn't have enough cream cheese for your favorite frosting? And this is the thanks I get?"

In addition to feeling hurt ourselves, it's natural to want to make a case for why our spouses shouldn't have felt hurt, or for how they should have handled things differently. "I didn't ignore you on your birthday! I don't know why you're so thin-skinned. Remember, I tried to draw you into the conversation my family was having around the table. *You're* the one who left the room to check on the kids and then didn't come back for forty-five minutes. How can you expect to feel a part of things?"

Even though it is quite natural, it's not very helpful to take our spouses' feelings personally and become defensive. It's much more helpful to acknowledge their feelings and treat them as valid. Simply see where they are emotionally and join them there by empathizing. However, even when we get that far, there are pitfalls to beware of. We may conclude that we are to blame for their distress, for example, when in actuality another person's feelings are usually not our fault. Very little good can come from such a conclusion as, "Sorry I ruined your birthday."

We also may erroneously decide that, in order to treat feelings as legitimate and important, we need to soothe them or make things better: "Let's go out to dinner this weekend, just you and me. You'll have my full, undivided attention. Next year, in addition to the cake, I'll make your favorite meal, too. We'll make it your best birthday ever." Again, not necessary.

When Earl talked to Carolyn, to her credit, she listened with compassion as he described how he had felt. The main thing we need when we're feeling bad is for someone important to us to willingly take in what we're feeling and simply try to understand what we're going through. "Oh, honey," she said when he finished, "I didn't realize that you were feeling that way." She looked him in the eye and reached over and pressed her palm on the side of his neck. "I can see it now. I can understand why you got feeling unimportant."

This process of acknowledging and validating the other's emotions will sound familiar because it's exactly what we recommended earlier that men can do to help their wives heal from the trauma they've experienced. It's exactly what wives need from husbands in everyday life when they're feeling bad. This commonality is not so surprising; these are universal human needs.

In fact, when Earl told me about how Carolyn responded, I thought of the incident on the swing set with my daughter. She wasn't that different from Earl. It didn't help when I said to her, "I'll push you some more." It didn't help when I explained that she needed to take turns with her sibling. It wouldn't have helped even if I had promised to be the best dad ever for the rest of her life. Her distress wasn't primarily about me anyway, it was about her. She was feeling distraught over being ignored. She finally felt heard and was able to calm down when I empathized with her. She then knew that I knew how she was feeling. She could see that I had allowed it in, and the little part in her brain that was blaring like a smoke alarm finally got the feedback it needed: *He knows what I'm feeling. I'm not alone in it anymore.* She had the emotional oxygen she needed to turn her attention to other things. She was ready to have me watch her go down the slide.

Not long ago a colleague told me about a video on YouTube of a tantruming little boy. The first thing you see is a boy crying on the floor. Video camera in hand, his mother stands up and walks out of the room. The tantrum stops as the boy stands up to come see where Mommy went. As soon as he comes into her line of sight (and into view of the camera) again, he drops to the floor with a wail. After a moment, she backs around another corner. The result is the same: silence until she reappears, and then he immediately tumbles to the floor again in tears.

I would have laughed harder at the video except that it reminded me of how I am when I'm physically ill. I don't moan in pain, even if I'm in pain, unless my wife is within earshot. When we're hurting, we want to know that someone we care about knows and cares that we feel bad.

One of our sons had a hard time talking to me and his mom when he was upset as a young child. However, he didn't just keep his feelings in. He would go find a pencil and paper and make a sketch for us. Here's one that we saved (see below). He would bring it in and wait for us to acknowledge its meaning. Then, and only then, it seemed, he could move on.

There are still times when we feel just like my son did when he drew this picture. It's painful to feel that way, but even more awful is to feel all alone when we're swamped by such feelings. Take the risk of reaching out. As we tell our kids, "Use your words!" If you're not going to talk, at least draw your spouse a picture! Sure, it may feel like you are at risk of being seen as more of a wimp than you've ever been before, but you'll be a lot less vulnerable to the pull of porn.

Reaching out for emotional closeness and soothing may feel especially risky if there have been years of conflict with your partner. Nonetheless, plowing through whatever struggle you have to in order to connect is your best option for optimal health and growth. Ed Tronick, a professor of child development, explains, "We thrive in the messiness of human connection. Without it, we wither" (Tronick 2008, 5). Being alone and isolated is ultimately worse for us than the short-term struggle to regain connection in our attachment relationships.

SHE'S YOUR BEST GUIDE IN THE UNFAMILIAR REALM OF EMOTIONS

Jerry had been free of problems with pornography for just over a year. His wife, Wendy, still felt insecure about his recovery and frequently checked in with him about it. One Friday night as he walked in the house after work, Wendy said, "You had a problem today, didn't you"—meaning a relapse to pornography.

After doing well for so long, Jerry had begun to wonder how long he would have to be on track before she'd have more confidence in him. To his credit, however, instead of getting exasperated, he went over, put his hand on her shoulder, looked her in the eye, and earnestly said, "I haven't. It's still going well, honey."

Wendy responded, "It's just that you have that same look about you—that vacant look in your eyes you used to get when you were caught up in your addiction." She paused for a minute, then asked, "Is there something else going on for you?"

Jerry sighed and shrugged. "I don't know. I didn't think so."

"Well, I think it would be worth exploring a bit, don't you?"

Jerry shrugged again. "Maybe, but you're going to have to help walk me through it."

They went into their bedroom together and he lay down. She sat next to him on the edge of the bed. "How was work for you today?"

"It was all right. Pretty good, in fact. I mean, it's Friday, so I was looking forward to the weekend."

"No stresses about your deadline next week? No run-ins with coworkers or management?"

"Things are going fine, really."

"Was there anything else that was on your mind today?"

"Like I said, I'm looking forward to the weekend. Tomorrow should be nice. We'll take care of the yard in the morning, go to the kids' soccer games, and still have some time to relax. And then Sunday . . . I'm really honored that Bensons have asked me to be the one to offer the prayer when we all get together to pray for Roger. I'm so glad my life's back on track again so that I feel worthy to offer spiritual support when people are in need. It means a lot to me that they asked. His entire extended family will be fasting. He told me last week that both of their parents will be there, and his brother will be in town from Arizona."

Jerry paused for a moment. "I hope that goes well. I'm looking forward to it, but at the same time it is intimidating. I hope that I say the right things—that I'm in tune with the Spirit. I feel clean and capable of receiving inspiration, but I hope . . . I want it to be everything they've been hoping and praying for. I love them so much and want so badly for the Lord to bless their family. They've put their trust in the Lord and in me. I know God will be there for them, but I really don't want to let them down on my end. I guess my confidence in my spirituality has taken some hits over the last few years.

"Oh . . ." Jerry let out a long sigh, and then he laughed. "Yeah, that's it! That's what's been building up inside. I care so much about Roger and his family. I want so much for the Lord to bless them. I don't want them to suffer anymore. I don't want to let them down. They've suffered so much disappointment already. I hope that I can be strong in my faith, for their sake. Yeah, that's what I've been concerned about. That's what's eating at me."

Wendy, relaxed now, was nodding her head as she lightly patted Jerry's chest. Jerry sat up and hugged her. "Thank you, sweetie. Oh, man, you know where I'm coming from. You know how afraid I get that I'll let people down. But wow, ahhh. It sure feels a lot better to talk it out."

It does feel better to talk out our feelings. And, as we so often remind clients, if you don't *talk out* your feelings, you're leaving yourself at risk of *acting out* on them.

HELPING EACH OTHER HEAL OLD WOUNDS

It was midnight, and Tim was pacing around his motor home. The fire had long ago died out. Dinner was lukewarm in the Dutch oven. Sylvia had made the three-hour drive from their remote campsite back to town the night before so that she could spend the day catching up on some crucial things at work, but she'd planned on being back by dinnertime. Tim didn't think she'd been in an accident on the way back, but there was no way for him to be sure. All his calls were going straight to voice mail. He tried not to think about the three men he'd caught her corresponding with by e-mail and exchanging explicit chat messages with. Despite his efforts, however, some of the things one of them had said to her had popped into his mind: "We'd be great together. You really ought to move out to Florida so that we can make a go of it."

At first Tim had felt so crushed by the revelation that he had contemplated ending his own life. Of course, it was partly about those relationships, but there was even more to it. He'd been vulnerable to the fear of abandonment before he'd ever gotten together with Sylvia. Since the discovery of Sylvia's virtual affairs a few months ago, he'd spent a lot of time working to become more aware of the connection between his overwhelming emotional reaction to her behavior and similar feelings from earlier in his life. He had been a handful to his parents as a child and remembered listening to them argue over his custody. In his case, for as long as he could remember, each of them wanted Tim to live with the *other* one. Finally, he had gotten into a fistfight with his younger half brother at his mom's house. That and some other acting up and involvement with the law had led to his removal from his parents' custody and placement at age fifteen in the first of a series of foster homes.

Tim now knew that he was more prone as an adult to feeling rejected, abandoned, and worried that he had to face the world alone because of those early experiences. That knowledge didn't necessarily help him feel better now as he gazed out into the silent black Wyoming sky, but it helped him at least make sense of the lump in his throat and the ache in his heart.

Tim didn't have a way of knowing exactly how out of proportion his feelings were about the current situation. However, he'd talked with Sylvia quite a bit about his feelings in the past and she'd been understanding and supportive. Therefore, when she finally arrived at quarter after one, he felt free to simply pour out his soul to her: his worry, his impatience, the way the time had stretched on and had become an eternity, his anger, his love and feelings of need for her, and, scariest of all, his fear that she had left and wasn't coming back.

Sylvia informed him briefly about the extra work that had been piled on her and the dead cell-phone battery, but she didn't get defensive or minimize his emotional reaction. The beef stew remained untouched in the fire pit as she held his hands in hers and listened attentively to all of Tim's hurt and fear. They talked about the feelings that were fresh, but also about the deeper, long-ago wounds that had been reopened by the day's events.

They finally ate and went to bed an hour or so later. At 5:00 a.m. Tim woke up in the middle of a nightmare. He woke up Sylvia and described reliving in his dream the moment when he had realized that he had to use his first foster family's bathroom supplies. He shared a bathroom with their two boys, and for some reason it really bugged him that he was going to be using their shampoo and soap. Then he cried as he recalled his first Christmas in foster care, away from his family. His mom had waited until Christmas evening to call and talk to him. He hadn't heard from his dad at all. He remembered having that same lump in his throat, the one that had been there before Sylvia had arrived back at camp, that entire first holiday season he spent living in the home of strangers.

Sylvia squeezed Tim tighter and rocked gently forward and back as she told him how sorry she was that he had experienced that. How much she knew it had hurt him. How tenderhearted she knew he had always been underneath the hardened shell of a rebellious teenager. Tim didn't remember falling asleep, but the next morning he felt that there had been lifted from him a burden, the weight of which he hadn't before even realized.

It's counterintuitive to view moments marked by raw emotion as great opportunities for bonding. We wouldn't see them that way ourselves except for hearing from couples like Tim and Sylvia about experiences like this. It is tough, but couples can start to see such moments this way and resist the impulse to go back to their old conflict-ridden patterns. Then, when they're honest with themselves and their spouses about their most tender feelings, their spouses can give free rein to their own nurturing instincts. This is when hurts that are even older than their relationship, hurts that are an entire lifetime old, can be soothed and can start to be healed.

OVER TIME, IT BECOMES LESS AND LESS ABOUT SEX

Dwight had been excited for his business trip to Chicago for a professional conference ever since he'd been promoted. The first morning at the convention hall there was a lot of backslapping and friendly greetings. These people all seem to know each other, Dwight thought. He wondered if he stood out as a new guy. He felt out of place. As the morning went on, he started to worry that maybe his boss had intended him to be doing the kind of socializing and networking that everybody else there seemed to be doing. He wondered, "Am I not cut out to be a product manager after all?" He remembered, to his relief, that in the afternoon there would be a breakout session with just a handful of people from around the country with job descriptions like his. He was more comfortable in small groups.

Almost immediately in that meeting he started to feel like he was in over his head. "I should have finished my degree," he thought. He made a comment, but it seemed to fall flat and the discussion moved right past the topic he brought up. By the end of the afternoon his neck muscles were taut and his chest was starting to ache. It was going to be a long three days. By dinnertime he was looking forward to the chance to relax on his own and get a bite to eat. Seated at his table in the restaurant, as the stress was just starting to melt away, a large group of people, some of whom he recognized from the convention, was ushered to a cluster of tables right beside him. A couple of the people glanced his way and seemed to recognize him. He sat quietly and ate as they chatted and joked and laughed together.

As he left the restaurant to walk back to his hotel, Dwight called Vaughn, his Sexaholics Anonymous sponsor. "Trip's not going exactly as I'd hoped." When he got back to his room and into bed, he called his wife, Karen.

"How's it going there, honey?" she asked.

"Not too well," Dwight said, feeling tight in his chest and throat again. It was quiet on the line for a moment.

"Are you okay?"

"Yeah . . . sorry," he said, getting even more choked up. "I guess I'm just . . . I miss you guys . . . being away from home. Plus, it really caught me by surprise, how unsure of myself I feel here. Like a fish out of water. Everyone seems so on the ball. I'm just, well . . . me."

Softly, Karen said, "Ohhhh, honey. I'm sorry it's been a hard day for you." They were both quiet. Finally Karen continued, "I wish I could be with you there right now. I'd just wrap my arms around you and tell you how much we appreciate you going out there, slaying the dragon to take care of us. We're cozy and happy here and you're going through the tough stuff to keep us that way."

Dwight laughed through tears that had welled up. "It seems a little silly that it's tough to sit through a couple of meetings and check out some booths, but I guess it has been today."

Karen promised to check in with him midway through the next morning. After he said good night to the kids and hung up the phone, the emotion that had been building up all day was still right there, ready to overflow. Dwight let it come. He put his head in his hands and sobbed. He wiped his eyes and blew his nose and then cried again. For a couple of minutes the tears flowed. As they subsided, he felt spent but relaxed and, in a way, clear. As if he'd cleaned out the gunk that had been building up. That night, he said, he slept like a baby.

He awoke early the next morning feeling rested and refreshed. That day at the convention wasn't a picnic either, by any means, but he recalled later that he felt a little lighter, freer to be himself. He regretted that he was not more socially skilled, and his lack of ease and grace hit home to him again a couple of times, but he felt a bit less tense about it. He knew he wasn't perfect, but he didn't feel quite as much pressure to be. He noticed at the end of the day that he was breathing freer and didn't feel nearly as uptight as he had the night before.

I first heard about his business trip from the counselor who leads the therapy group Dwight attends. When I did, all I could think about was Sherlock Holmes and "The Curious Incident of the Dog in the Night-Time."

You might remember that story: A thief stole a prized horse from the stable. While everyone else was looking for clues the thief may have left behind—what's here now that wasn't before?—the master detective was thinking about what *hadn't* happened that should have. Specifically, no one had heard anything out of the ordinary. And yet, there was the dog, calm and seemingly un-molested. Holmes's conclusion: The thief must have been some-one the dog knew. With the pool of suspects sufficiently narrowed, the thief was discovered straightaway.

What was the dog that didn't bark in the night for Dwight? During that trip and in his description of it afterward, he never brought up the topic of pornography. He hadn't viewed pornog-raphy, but neither had he experienced a craving for pornography worth mentioning. He hadn't had to resist with all of his might some potent urge to view pornography. He had simply been willing to acknowledge what he was going through, stay with his feelings even though they were distressing, and talk about them.

161

I asked Dwight how different this was from the way he would have handled the same feelings before he was in recovery. "I know exactly how I would have handled them, because I used to travel all the time. I would have sneered at 'all of these shallow people who act like they're best friends with these business associates they only see twice a year.' I would have tried to convince myself that I was better than them for not being so slick: 'I'm no used car salesman.' I don't know that I would have admitted to myself that I felt bad that I'm not as smooth and charismatic as I'd like to be. I'm sure I wouldn't have lasted the day. I would have snuck away to go golfing or at least sightseeing, probably missing big chunks of the convention in order to avoid staying there and feeling out of place. Then I would have had to figure out how to cover up that missed time when I reported back to my boss."

Feelings like the ones he'd had on that trip had surely always been there, building up for Dwight. How would things have gone had he not recognized the strong feelings he was having and dealt with them for what they were? He had many trips to look back on and see how it would have gone. In the past, things had always escalated until he eventually succumbed to his addictive behaviors.

I thought about Karen's nurturing, soothing response on the phone. I thought about how comforting that must have been for Dwight to hear in his moment of greatest need. He was primed, receptive, and in need of connection and renewal, and she didn't disappoint. Throughout his earlier years of travel, he had been in just as great a need. However, he didn't know what he needed, and he certainly didn't know how to reach out to Karen for it. In fact, nine months earlier, in his first few weeks of recovery, he had gone on a business trip to Texas. He hadn't yet learned to identify what he was going through emotionally and stay with it instead of distracting himself from it or trying to escape it. Therefore, he couldn't talk with Karen about it. He was honest with her when they talked on the phone during that trip and admitted that he had a harder time resisting temptation on the road than he did at home. Her response? "I'm here on my own day and night taking care of your children and you're off engaged and interacting with other people during the day and then at night you can't help wanting to think about having sex with other women?" She didn't say the next part out loud, but to herself Karen even wondered, *What kind of a creep did I marry?*

Karen didn't marry a creep. She married a man who would, nine months later, elicit a very different response in her: "Ohhhh, honey. You love us so much. You are *my* man, out there slaying dragons. You take care of us so well. We're so secure here because of you." She responded differently because he was able to reveal to her the real Dwight. He was the same man, having much the same experience, but he had learned to choose connection—to himself and to his wife—over addiction. And he didn't long for the old days. He didn't have to white-knuckle his way through temptation. In his heart of hearts he much preferred the path he was on.

What went on within Dwight—deep down, emotionally—was a fresh revelation not only to Karen but to Dwight himself. He had learned in his recovery that to overcome his double life, he had to not only be honest about his behavior but rooted in and true to his emotions. Only when he was real with himself could he be real with Karen.

I keep Dwight and Karen in mind when I work with couples who are in the beginning stages of dealing with a pornography habit that has been kept secret. It helps me remember the kind of relationship couples can have—if they keep working at it. Early on, she may be tempted to leave because of how badly she's been hurt and how little compassion he seems to have for her pain. He may be tempted to give up on the relationship because of how ashamed he feels and how little hope he has of ever making things better between them again and finally being the man she really wants.

However, I remind myself that a pornography problem can be a cancer in a relationship that has a lot of other strengths and reasons to survive. The problem is not the body—the couple's relationship. Each spouse may have admirable intentions and strengths. It's so much easier to connect with the tender, feeling person who is behind the reactive behavior and words that are so often all we see from the surface.

Nonetheless, cancer can do terrible things to even the healthiest of bodies. Dwight was not a terrible guy who didn't think about or care about his wife. And yet the pornography habit made him exactly that in her mind. Fortunately, when couples are willing to draw together and risk being tender and real with each other, healing can happen and closeness can return.

CHAPTER 7

Porn Is No Match for Real Connection

Healing your relationship isn't just about getting over pornography. You can get over a porn habit, and your partner can get over his or her hard feelings about it, and yet you still might not have a deeply rewarding relationship. The healthiest outcome isn't simply to produce two recovered individuals. Instead, think of this crisis of pornography as an invitation to learn a new and authentic form of intimacy with your partner.

Turning toward pornography for comfort and relief was nothing more than movement away from your most important relationship. As you face a new direction, leave the pull of pornography, and watch your partner take risks to trust again, your new trajectories set both of you up for emotional connections previously unavailable.

Don't miss this opportunity and settle for "good enough" in something so profoundly important. The goal isn't to just stop the harmful habits. The connection and closeness you share with your beloved can become the most fulfilling aspect of your life. It can be your greatest treasure.

In this chapter, we'll describe the case of Alex and Tonya, a couple who are pulling off this very thing. Then, at the end of the chapter, we'll talk about how to avoid the pitfalls that can prevent the deepening of emotional intimacy. We'll also help you develop some practices—think of them as healthy rituals—that will keep your relationship-building efforts on track.

Alex was discouraged about the rate of progress in his relationship with his wife, Tonya. Even though he hadn't acted out sexually for eleven months, she still seemed distant, disinterested, even disconnected. It was almost as though, during the time he had been so caught up in his addiction, she had come to terms with his emotional absence and moved on with her life without him.

I could see that Alex's heart ached as he talked about the loss of what they'd had before. "I'm coming to believe that we'll never get back to the friendship and closeness we once shared—or anything near it. She used to refer to me as 'my miracle' to her friends. I loved her kids, solved her financial problems. But I worry whether she'll ever be able to be happy with a knight in tarnished armor."

Over the previous year and a half, Alex had made tremendous progress in his individual recovery. He had learned to sit through his cravings when they hit instead of locking horns with them. At first it was hard for him to maintain his attention on this inner process that had always gotten him into trouble, but he'd gotten better at it with practice. He had discovered that there was a life cycle to temptation and the feelings that came in its wake. He now knew that he if he waited them out, they would dissipate on their own. He practiced being mindful, or aware of the workings of his mind, rather than simply being carried along by his thoughts. Here were some of the waves that washed into his consciousness when he was tempted:

At first he would feel the excitement of, "I could go do that again. The good stuff is waiting right there for the taking."

When he just sat with that titillation, he noticed that the next wave quickly came, stirring up feelings of embarrassment, fear of the costs of that lifestyle, and a sense of loss over the price he had paid for his transgressions already.

As the tide of desire continued to rise, he would think, "It seems so gratifying, I'm going to lose control . . ." Again, in the wake of that wave he would notice a rejoinder: "but then I'll lose everything."

He thought back on those times when he had first practiced watching the tug-of-war in his mind and becoming more aware of its nature instead of entering wholeheartedly into it. "That's when it would seem that the losses I was going to suffer over this would devastate me. I had invited this boulder of sexual addiction into my life, and its impact was now rippling out and affecting everything: my family, my extended family, my business, my health. I knew that if I continued I would become a pitiful person, a loser. I'd be left with a sense of despair."

Simply sitting with all of those feelings allowed them to dissipate. Alex discovered that the tide didn't keep rising; it eventually ebbed. Thinking back on that work, he said, "I hadn't ever before realized that if I let those sexual cravings and other feelings come, one emotion would flow to another and eventually the ship would right itself without my having to put up much resistance. It was really helpful to stay with it and watch the feelings almost change themselves. Temptation, when it has occurred since, hasn't seemed as dangerous."

Earlier in life, Alex never would have suspected that he could experience this level of empowerment in the midst of an urge. For as long as he could remember, he had been waging a Herculean war against temptation. "It took so much white-knuckling. I would hum hymns to myself, quote poetry, think of my father being with me. Those were sometimes the only things that kept me from giving in, and sometimes then only by a thread. At times I would go five or ten years with no mistakes, but all the time battling, trying to control myself. Even when I was serving later as a lay leader in my church, the thoughts kept coming to me. I had to keep trying to keep all the feathers in the room, all the animals in the bag. As long as I had total focus, I was okay. But if the bag got a little hole and one of the animals squirmed out, I was in trouble. It was an even bigger fight. Eventually I dropped the bag. They all got loose. I stopped trying. I convinced myself that the boundaries I did maintain were important—such as no sexual intercourse outside my marriage—but looking back I can see that that was only to help myself feel better about what I was doing. I was committing adultery, no two ways about it. Having failed to conquer the compulsion, I was trying to accommodate it. Of course, that didn't work. Then it expanded at an even more accelerated pace. It was taking over my life. That was when I knew I had to talk to Tonya and get some help."

It had never occurred to Alex before coming to treatment that his sexual urges might arise from displaced emotional needs. However, when he thought back on his younger years, it made sense to him that he had gone to sex for comfort when he needed emotional connection and relationship soothing. He recalled how terrified he was the summer of his seventh year when his mother locked herself in her room for a week crying. That distinct feeling that he was on his own. Alex knew that she loved him and wanted what was best for him, but from then on he felt like he could never predict from one day to the next whether he could count on her to be there for him in times of need. He tried to be strong so as to not add to her burden. He became convinced at an early age that he had to take care of himself emotionally. When he discovered masturbation a short time later, sexual thoughts and feelings became a reliable standby that he would use to help himself feel calm enough to get to sleep at night, occupy himself when there was nothing else to do, pacify himself when his feelings were hurt, and generally alleviate unsettled feelings whenever he didn't know what else to do.

Now, he had learned that if he would sit and breathe long enough in the midst of a craving, it eventually faded, like a wave settling back into the sea. Then he could comb the still-moist beach of his consciousness for the remnants of the emotions that may have triggered the urge in the first place. "It was enlightening that as I just sat with sexual feelings, they would evolve into these other things," he said. Although he had been doing great work along these lines, he still stood at the frontier of the most important part of his recovery: the healing of his relationship with his wife. There's a huge difference between becoming aware of emotional needs and honoring those needs by building a genuine emotional connection with a real human being.

Reaching out is a huge risk because the beloved person to whom we are reaching doesn't always respond in the way we hope. It wasn't surprising to me that, in the beginning of his work, Alex reached out to Tonya sexually. It also didn't surprise me when Tonya rejected his advances. Here's what he said at that time: "She said she wasn't ready. 'Sorry, I just need some time.' I've been rejected by her several times recently. It hurts more to be rejected than to go without. I'm discouraged. I don't know if things will ever get better. I've decided not to approach her anymore. I don't need one more rejection with everything else going on."

The "everything else going on" that Alex referred to included cash flow problems for his business and an upcoming appointment

with the urologist. He had been checking in with the doctor an-
nually over the last few years because his PSA levels had been
elevated, raising the specter of prostate cancer. Two weeks later,
Alex's furrowed brow spoke volumes. "The levels were high
enough that they took a biopsy. My dad died of that cancer. He
didn't have his prostate removed and he ended up suffering the
last three years of his life. I'll probably have the surgery, but I've
talked with a couple of friends who've had it and it virtually ended
their sex lives. Because of the state of my relationship with Tonya
right now, I've given up on sexual intimacy."

Alex seemed to look past me. "I may have already had the last
intimate encounter I'll ever have in my life. What I've had so far
is all I'm going to get. Given my lack of hope for things improv-
ing with Tonya, mentally and emotionally I could almost go back
to acting out right now. Part of the temptation of illicit activity is
that there was no variety or spice with Tonya, even when we were
having sex. It was the same thing every time, so what incentive is
there to work to get back to that? And then I think that there's only
a slim possibility of it ever returning even to that. The only thing
that keeps me from trying to find a connection with someone else
is that she made it clear that that would be *it* for us. I do know that
she's a critical part of my life and my future. I have to give up the
thought that there's a better option outside our marriage, that it
would be better to start over fresh with someone else."

As he talked about his life with his wife, Alex seemed to come
back to his senses. "If I left her, there may not be anything else
that would keep me from being forever lost in the black hole of
addiction. It would be spiritual suicide. Plus, she does want the
relationship to work," he said with a sense of resolve, "and I just
can't risk losing her because I didn't do my part."

I referred Alex and his wife for marriage counseling with
a trusted colleague who helped Alex see that Tonya was not

disinterested in him or uncaring about their relationship at all, but rather was still aching. She had retreated from him to the safety of aloneness, not because she didn't love him, but because he mattered so much to her that she couldn't bear to be hurt again by him in the ways that she had been. She had put on a good face for the outside world. She had continued to play the part of a committed wife and involved member of their community and church. However, she carried within her now a deep pain that was never far from the surface.

During marriage counseling sessions, Tonya shared with Alex that she had long worried that he didn't want her but would rather have had someone younger and with a more perfect body. She feared that he was looking for someone he would prefer to her, and could easily dump her if and when he found that woman. Of course, this made sense to Alex, and he knew that this very worry might be going on inside her because of his struggles, but he comprehended her dread in a much more profound way as he sat across from her for ninety minutes at a time during those counseling sessions. He felt it more deeply when he looked her in the eyes as she described her pain and panic at the thought of losing him, the most important person in her life.

The counselor asked what she would need from Alex in order to feel differently, to be convinced over time that her fears weren't true, that he did want her, and that she wouldn't lose him. She said that the work he had done to recover from his sexual compulsions had helped, but for some reason it hadn't been enough. "Logically I know that he's working to avoid infidelity, but in some part of me . . . in my heart, I guess, I dread that maybe he's staying out of a sense of duty or to keep providing a solid home base for our kids and grandkids. Deep down I'm not convinced that he wants to be with me."

The counselor had watched Alex sit and patiently listen to

Tonya. He knew that Alex had been allowing her experience to impact him, really letting her feelings in. He had also seen the difference that had made for Tonya and knew that she might be more ready to ask for what she needed from her husband. Again the counselor asked what she needed from Alex, what he could do to help when she felt afraid that he didn't really want to be with her.

"He could come and spend time with me. Sit and hold me or hold hands with me at the end of the day. Talk about the day together. Knowing that he chooses to spend that time with me might help me feel like he really does want to be with me. It would be nice if I felt like he needed me, too, if I felt like what I do and offer and give makes a difference to him."

Over the next few months, Alex and Tonya got together and spent some time talking at the end of almost every day. They had some physical contact, such as holding hands, sitting side by side, and occasionally cuddling. They sat together or sometimes walked around the block. Alex was surprised how often the topic of feeling unwanted came up for Tonya. It got triggered in their relationship if he didn't ask her opinion on a decision or got working late and forgot to call. But she also felt pained when their daughter chose to stay with her friend when she was in town instead of staying at their place. It welled up when two of her friends in the neighborhood went to lunch without inviting her.

As Alex and Tonya sat together by the fireplace and talked throughout the coldest winter months of that year, Tonya began to feel freer, and their conversations ranged more widely. She revealed to Alex the pain of having wished that she could receive as much of her dad's attention as her two little brothers did. She recalled rubbing her fingers on the worn red velvet armrest of his easy chair, trying to will him to put down the newspaper that stood like a brick wall between them. She recalled the emptiness she had felt in her first marriage as her husband had moved from one exciting, unfruitful venture to another, always caught up in the anticipation of success and riches. He was always animated, but she was always in the background. There never seemed to be a place for her in his dreams.

As Tonya opened up her heart and shared these hurts, a heart-wrenching picture of her pain was becoming clearer and clearer to Alex. Most distressing of all to him was the role he could see that he played in deepening her wounds. On the one hand, he realized that his addiction was about him and his inability to cope well with his own emotional reactions and needs. On the other hand, he had always known that Tonya had taken his behavior as a personal rejection, and he thought he had understood why. There were enough obvious reasons. However, now he could see even more deeply. When he turned his attention to other women, even imaginary ones by way of pornography or anonymous prostitutes, he was subjecting Tonya to one more experience, in a long line of them, where she felt unwanted, uninteresting, easy to ignore . . . easily *resistable*. By that time in her life, it had left her feeling utterly discarded. As she put it: "I had fallen head-over-heels in love with you. I'd never felt adequate in the other most important relationships with men in my life. Finally, I was in a relationship where I was adequate—you let me know that I was enough for you and more. I thought that for our first ten years together. Then, to discover that I wasn't, that you had these other attractions . . . my world crumbled."

She was speaking to Alex frankly about how he had hurt her, and yet he didn't run away. He didn't even look away. He kept listening. He was there for her when she needed him the most, when she was feeling pain over the rejection she'd received from the one person who mattered most to her in his life: him. Tonya kept talking about her hurt, and she seemed to value tremendously the time they spent together in the evenings. Even though their conversation topics were often painful ones, Alex noticed that, as the weeks went on, she seemed brighter-eyed and quicker to smile. It occurred to Alex that his listening might be a key part of his making amends to her.

As I kept meeting with Alex, I could tell that his listening was not only affecting Tonya deeply, it was having a profound impact on him. "I've felt deeply the hurt I've caused her, and it hurts me. I'm so motivated not to ever do anything that would cause her that grief again—especially in light of the love she's expressed. Despite the pain and all we've been through, she has continued to hold this deep and abiding love for me," Alex said, shaking his head in amazement. Alex sat quietly then, in reverence over his wife's grace and resilience. I could tell that her feelings for him had become sacred to him.

A month or so later, Alex said, "We're connecting more sexually. It's not as spontaneous as it was in our earlier years; intimacy requires more preparation. But if I set the stage and I'm sensitive and thoughtful, I'm never met with rejection. I'm realizing that and learning that. Tonya is coming around and wanting to have all the connection we've had at previous times. She is wanting to be more careful and she's a bit guarded. But I know where that comes from and I honor its importance. It doesn't make me feel rejected or impatient, like it used to."

Alex also found it very healing to go to Tonya when he was in need. This was so different for him from how he had learned to handle things growing up. He had taken to heart his father's attitude about complaining. When they worked together in the yard and Alex would grumble, his dad would respond, "If you can't handle it out here, get in the house with your mom and sisters." This had helped him develop a great can-do mentality and a toughness that had served him well in most areas of life. However, he realized now that he had taken it too far by figuring he had to be

174

tough and to close off his emotions even in his most intimate relationship, where it was safe to express more vulnerability. He said
once, "I don't have to give up that warrior mentality . . . but even a
warrior needs at times to put down the shield, take off the armor,
and let someone care for him and nurse the wounds he's suffered
out on the field of battle."

If Alex lost a client at work and felt less wanted or needed,
he would talk to Tonya about it at the end of the day. When he
was worried about his health and had concerns about his medical
treatment, he would share with her his feelings of fear and vulnerability. During a messy period of conflict with a coworker, usually supportive colleagues and superiors seemed indifferent. He
suddenly felt lost at work, which was usually a comfortable place
for him. For a week and a half he couldn't wait to talk with Tonya
each night about how it was going—not just about the events but
about the frustrations, anxieties, and regrets that were triggered.
"Instead of just whining about the situation or dogging on people
at work, I was telling her about what was going on inside of me,
that I was feeling empty and disconnected and alone. It was such a
relief to be able to be real with my wife, to reach out and know she
would be there for me, even when it was really hard stuff. That's so
different for me from what I sometimes did before by running to
her and gossiping about work."

When Alex came home at the end of the day, bearing all his
cares and worn down by the troubles of life, it felt so good to be
met by Tonya's mild and easy attentiveness. The more he reached
out to her and found solace, the more he found that during the day
at work, when his mind started going to despair, he craved her affection and kindness. He knew that he could come home and pour
out to her everything he'd gone through during the day, holding
nothing back. He knew that she would share his burden. He knew

that her gentle voice would work all the kinks out of his heart and mind.

A month later, Alex told me that the progress in their physical relationship had stalled. "We've had nothing, sexually speaking, for a couple of months. I was impatient before, but now I'm realizing more and more her view. I'm content with the connections we *are* making." Before he went in for another PSA test to check on the growth of his prostate cancer, he told her, "We may not be able to have sex in the future, and I'm trying to be okay with that." Tonya was touched by that expression. It indicated to her that he was rising above his obsession with sex and his attempts to control that part of their relationship. Alex confided that he did occasionally have vivid dreams of Tonya coming to him and initiating affection.

Regarding urges and cravings, Alex said at that time, "I'm becoming more relaxed with respect to my destructive behavior. I still have the desire to look at porn or seek illicit sex from time to time, but it's not as often. A big part of what has softened it is having come to understand over the last couple of months more than I did before the pain I've caused Tonya. I regret having ever lectured her about forgiveness. No explanation, talking, or recitation of scripture is going to affect her. If anything will, it's my being attentive, swallowing my pride, and attempting to be close. I may be rejected, but only for now. For a while I told her that I was leaving it up to her to initiate physical contact so that she could wait until she was ready. At the time I convinced myself that I was doing that to avoid putting pressure on her or putting her in an uncomfortable situation. However, as time went on and I got real with myself, I could see that I was doing that as a cop-out, almost a punishment. I need to keep reaching out."

Alex went back to expressing physical affection, but he took baby steps instead of giant leaps. He looked for opportunities to hug Tonya, hold her hand, and rub her feet or her back. Eventually, she thanked him for that. She softened and expressed gratitude for his persistence. "Even when I've been a cold fish, you kept letting me know you wanted things to be better." She acknowledged then that she had been afraid of responding too soon to his efforts. She hadn't wanted to "let him off the hook" and let him think that what he'd done wasn't as big a deal as it was to her. She hadn't wanted to give the impression that she wasn't upset and hurt. Alex knew that Tonya had been holding back, so that wasn't news to him. Nonetheless, it felt good to hear her acknowledge that she wasn't coming in his direction, and to understand why.

Later Alex reported, "My time with Tonya is getting better and better all the time. Our focus has turned from my sexual problem. That hardly ever comes up anymore. Even when my indiscretions do come up, before long she dismisses the topic and moves on. Sort of like, 'We've already talked about that and worked through it.' Now we spend a lot more time talking about her depression, the difficulty she has being motivated and happy about anything. She always feels like she's not enough. That thought goes through her mind constantly. I offer her compliments, but she struggles to accept them. Now, gradually, she seems to be taking more in, but she's felt the other way for so many years. She talks a lot about her youth. Her father never encouraged or praised her. She said, 'I've never felt like I was able to be what I was supposed to be.' She felt like she couldn't keep men happy. Even God: she felt like she was a disappointment to her Heavenly Father. It broke my heart when I heard that, because there isn't a kinder, gentler person on the face of his earth.

"She's been singing for forty-plus years, but she has always focused on her mistakes and shortcomings after she performs. The last time she tried to sing, it was in church. I didn't hear a problem with it at all, but she sure did. She felt like she failed, and she also felt like God had let her down. He knew how badly she wanted to do well, and that she was doing it with a worshipping heart. She has talked to me over and over again about how devastating it is to feel abandoned and unwanted by God. I'm just listening and trying to support her and let her know that I hear her and feel for her over how hard that is. I've learned not to try to talk her out of it or sweep those feelings away."

Over the year and a half I had worked with Alex, I'd never seen him cry, but he was choking up and tearing up now. "I need to be there for her when she feels so discarded. I just have to keep making sure that I'm there for her when she's feeling so vulnerable, that I'm there for her when she needs me to be. She needs to feel God's touch and tenderness. She's missing it so much. If I can play any role in that, if she can feel His hand reaching out and touching her through my presence or attentiveness, I want desperately to help provide that for her."

A month later when we met, Alex said, "Tonya and I are more cuddly, touchy. We seek out each other before either of us leaves or when we get back to the house. We're not really home until we've touched base with each other. We talk in bed at night. We've been leaving the TV off and taking time to just hold each other." They'd taken a trip to Montana and stayed in a cabin on a remote lake. "After we got back from that getaway Tonya said that it was the happiest she can remember ever feeling," Alex recalled with a contented smile. "We were in the moment, enjoying each other. There were no pressures: the phones didn't work, we didn't have e-mail. We were nestled in this huge old-growth forest. We took long walks on the shore holding hands. Our relationship, our intimacy, our communication, our concern for each other— everything's been growing very well. We pulled our chairs up to the picture window looking out over the lake and held hands while I read a book and she worked on Sudoku puzzles."

Later in that session, when we were talking about his individual recovery, Alex said, "Because of how close we are and my sense of the affect my behavior has had on her, temptations don't have much impact on me these days. That's been one of the biggest changes. I had little sense before of the impact my behavior had on her. I had convinced myself that it was only affecting me. Before this process, I didn't realize the pain it created for Tonya. I honestly believed in the early stages that she didn't care that much. Particularly with the masturbation: I had convinced myself that it was a personal thing that didn't hurt anyone else."

Fast-forwarding another month, Alex reported, "The assignments we received in marriage counseling have become standard practice in our relationship. We take time every evening to talk and hold each other. We make a bigger deal of the hellos and good-byes, good mornings and good nights. I go find her when I get home and make a point of reconnecting. I didn't realize what a big deal those moments had become until I came home one afternoon and couldn't find her. She usually leaves a note, but this time she hadn't expected me to get back before she did. A couple of her friends in the neighborhood had come over and talked her into going on a walk with them. I tell you, I was walking around that house like a lost puppy. I was so glad when she got home and I could see her, give her a hug, and check in about the day.

"The gradual shift has continued, and now in our conversations there's even less focus on the sexual mistakes I've made. Now it's about us and about her never feeling like she's enough, and the way my behavior a year and a half ago reinforced that. We had a very good relationship when we were dating and courting and during the first part of our marriage, but it has new depth now. I don't think I *understood* her the way I do now. As horrible as my behavior was, something good has come from it. It has strengthened us and helped us get closer emotionally. Maybe that's the way it is—whenever someone's with you through experiences like that, you get closer. My love and appreciation is greater now because she's been there for me in my hardship. And now she's grateful because I'm there for her in her struggle.

"She deserves to feel better about herself. She's the only one who sees herself as inadequate; everyone else sees her as good and accomplished. Most of the time I just listen and try to understand, but some of the time I can't help sharing my feelings about her. She's getting better at taking compliments. I'm almost grateful that she has a bit of this struggle so that I can be a part of the solution and show her my gratitude for helping me solve my issues. We plan to renew our wedding vows in a couple of years, once my disciplinary process with our church is complete. It will be a nice chance to recommit. I'm hoping that it might be a breakthrough for her to realize I was willing to go through whatever process I needed to in order to be with her forever. I so want her to have the confidence that she is enough."

At the end of the session, Alex summed it up: "Things are progressing well. I was impatient in the beginning, but now I have a better understanding of how difficult the things she's working on are. I know they can't be rushed."

It was a couple of months before we met again, and Alex still appeared to be at ease. "Tonya had surgery. It was a good experience to be there waiting on her. I love her and want so much to be for her what she truly deserves. I did the big weekly dinner for our kids and grandkids on Sunday—cut up potatoes and put the roast in the Crock-Pot. My daughters brought a salad and dessert. For three or four days she was in bed and I looked after her. I stayed home from work during those mornings. I would help her get going and wash her wound, put ointment on it, and cover it with fresh bandaging. Twice a day I'm her nurse like that. She is so appreciative and feels bad that I have to take the time away from work. I don't feel bad at all—it's bonding for us to have this experience together. It's so different now, so much better. It makes me excited about the future."

Finally, I asked Alex about how he felt his individual recovery was going. "I don't feel much of a pull back to the addiction," he responded. "The strengthening of our relationship is probably the reason I don't feel any need to seek validation or intimacy anywhere else. We don't have sex as much as I'd like, partly due to Tonya's health issues. I'm fine with that because the emotional connection is so close. We are the best of friends. We enjoy spending time together. She keeps talking about our vacation in Montana, saying 'It was the best vacation we've ever had.' We've backpacked in New Zealand, sailed in the Caribbean, and been to some other exotic places. This one was different because we were close and open with each other. I enjoyed it as much as she did. The connection between us has expanded, and that, in turn, has totally deflated, totally taken away any pressure to go back to the destructive behavior. It's been months since I've even had a desire to masturbate or go back to worse stuff than that. In a way, I've been mystified by the loss of that appetite, and in fact at times almost frightened by the lack of urge. I've wondered if perhaps I had a new medical problem. I've never been here before. Throughout my life, as far back as I can remember, I've had that compulsive drive. Now I'll feel sexual feelings here and there and realize that I haven't lost the ability to have them, which is a relief in a way. However, they don't feel imperative; they're not obligatory. It feels so liberating to not have my life dominated by sexual thoughts and compulsions."

CREATING DAILY OPPORTUNITIES FOR CLOSENESS AND CONNECTION

We want to join together as partners to create the kind of relationship that will nourish us. To do so, we need to change more than just the patterns in our lives that were associated with the pornography use. True healing demands a deeper lifestyle change.

Before they ever had issues with pornography, many of those who have struggled had other habits and patterns—sources they would draw upon for emotional soothing. And if they're reaching for something else when they're in need, they're not reaching for their spouses.

Here's the way one client, Roland, put it: "I had a pre-addiction addiction. Before I was hooked on porn, I was overly dependent on TV and movies and the Internet—any and all forms of electronic media. I was always plugged in. Then eventually I would get plugged in to get turned on. I'm realizing that I have to do things differently now than I ever have before. I can't stay plugged in to the degree I was before and just avoid the getting-turned-on part. As I stay close to my wife in the process of recovery, I'm realizing that I have to be careful not to leave my worst habit behind— porn—only to go back to my pre-addiction addiction."

To keep building his relationship, Roland had to remind himself to slow down and become more conscious and deliberate about what he would do at the end of the day and on the weekends. At first it was a challenge to restrict how much he went to his smart phone, his various computers, and television. He had to guard against the drift back to old habits once the conflicts with his wife, Wanda, had settled down.

He found it valuable to read a written reminder about his most important priorities before he started his drive home from work. He found that the stress from the day would put him into an "autopilot" mentality, which would cause him to be emotionally unavailable to Wanda and the kids. After sitting down in his car, Roland would read the following: "It's not a crime to be tired after a long day at the office. But the people you are about to speak with are far more important than any client, colleague, or insurance-company employee you have spoken with today. Don't take for granted those you are going home to" (Felder 2005). This reminder interrupted the regular patterns that kept him disconnected from his most important relationships.

The rituals that create and maintain a pornography habit are often hard to detect at first. However, after pornography use has disappeared, it is easier to see the patterns that create disconnection and distance in the relationship.

Rather than leaving it to chance, we can be purposeful about setting up opportunities for closeness and connection. We can plug relationship-building rituals into our lives on a daily basis.

Bill Doherty, a marriage and family therapy professor at the Univeristy of Minnesota, has written extensively about marriage rituals as a way to safeguard marriages against what he calls "marital drift." He says: "I work in St. Paul, Minnesota, which is right near the Mississippi, the farthest north where big ships can navigate the river. Getting married, I say, is like getting into a canoe in the Mississippi River at St. Paul. If you don't paddle, you go south. Not that I have anything against the South, but if you don't want to go there, you've got a problem. If you want to stay at St. Paul, you've got to paddle. And if you want to go north, you have to have a plan. To grow closer over the years, you have to be mindful and intentional not only because of the pace and distractions of life, but also because of what research has shown is the loss of intensity that occurs from daily living over many months and years" (Doherty 1999).

Remember that pornography habits are highly ritualized. All of the behaviors leading up to the viewing of pornography, along with the actual acting-out behaviors, are repetitive and predictable. These rituals have to be replaced with healthier rituals that build connection and intimacy instead of isolation and distance.

Attachment relationships are formed on predictability and

LOVE YOU, HATE THE PORN

routine. Parents understand the need for building a secure ritual with their children, but sometimes it's hard to make the transition to doing this with adult relationships. For example, bedtime routines for children are essential for helping children relax and get a good night's sleep. These needs for rituals and predictability with a primary attachment figure don't magically disappear when we become adults.

When couples recognize their need for ongoing rituals of connection, unexpected things begin to happen. Trust begins to build, emotions are calmer, touch begins to return, and a general sense of well-being and safety begins to emerge.

Below are some ideas for ways to begin implementing relationship rituals with your partner. Mark the ones you want to start and feel free to add others that you come up with on your own.

Greeting and Parting Rituals
- Making a point of connecting when coming and going
- Embracing and kissing before leaving home
- Embracing and kissing on arrival home
- Knowing one thing your partner will be doing that day
- Asking one another about how the day went
- Using pet phrases that have meaning for you as a couple

Talk Rituals
- Checking in throughout the day
- Touching base when one or the other arrives home
- Sharing pillow talk at night before falling asleep (instead of watching TV)
- Reading articles or books to each other and discussing them
- Laughing together at the end of the day about enjoyments or stresses

- Sharing "highs and lows"—the best and worst things that happened that day
- Sharing not only the events but inner feelings that accompanied those experiences

Touch Rituals

- Embracing
- Kissing—especially lingering kisses
- Running fingers through hair
- Kissing the hand, neck, or forehead
- Spooning in bed
- Scratching backs
- Rubbing shoulders
- Massaging feet
- Placing hand on spouse's leg when sitting or driving
- Resting hand on partner's back or behind neck

Miscellaneous Rituals (may not occur daily)

- Going for walks
- Lying next to each other outside (under the stars, in the sun)
- Going out to eat
- Sitting together on a porch swing or love seat
- Going for a drive
- Sharing a snack before bedtime
- Singing
- Attending church
- Working side by side in the garden or yard

Keep deepening, nurturing, and protecting your relationship as a couple. When uncomfortable emotions surface for either partner, practice reaching toward each other for real relief. Then the pull of pornography will diminish for you and the pain of pornography will fade for your spouse. And while you will remove the cancer of pornography from your relationship, that won't be the primary benefit you'll be thinking about three months from now, three years from now, three decades from now. As you both invest time and energy in activities that feed and nurture your relationship, here's the primary benefit you'll enjoy: You'll be strengthening a bond that will nurture both of you forever.

ACKNOWLEDGMENTS

We want to express our sincere thanks to wonderful mentors, colleagues, and clients who have helped us learn what we've tried to teach in this book. Jack Boden has been a selfless teacher and mentor. The last chapter of this book could not have been written had Jack not done such great work with "Alex and Tonya."

Thanks to Rod Jeppsen and the whole crew at ARCH, and Jeff Ford and everyone else at LifeSTAR St. George, for wonderful friendships and collaboration. We've also gained so much over the years from our association with everyone at the Salt Lake Counseling Center and LifeSTAR Network—many thanks to Dan Gray, Todd Olson, Scott Peterson, Dorothy Maryon, Steve Johnson, and John Murdock.

Thanks to Dean Byrd for always being there in times of need. Thanks to Kevin Skinner, Rory Reid, and Laura Brotherson for all of your insights and your passion for helping couples in need. Thanks to Mark Kastleman for sharing the passion and the rest of the folks at Candeo for your creative efforts to send a lifeline to so many in need. Thanks to Craig Berthold, Jeff Robinson, Guerry Green, Phil and Colleen Harrison, Michael Gardner, and Craig Georgianna: We appreciate your bold ideas and dedication to helping people heal from addiction.

We want to acknowledge the contributions of Sue Johnson, Rebecca Jorgensen, Scott Wooley, and others in the Emotionally Focused Couples Therapy community who have taught and mentored us.

To Jana Erickson, Emily Watts, Chris Schoebinger, and the entire team at Shadow Mountain: Thanks for your tireless efforts. It's a pleasure to work with you.

To our clients: We admire your courage and appreciate your trust and patience. Thank you for letting us walk alongside you for part of your journey.

Finally, it would be impossible to write a book about attachment without being grateful to loving parents and siblings for "being there" and providing a solid and secure emotional foundation. Words cannot adequately express our gratitude.

Finally, to our wives, Jenny and Jody, and our children: Thank you for your undying love and support, through thick and thin. Helen Keller said, "What we have once enjoyed we can never lose. All that we love becomes a part of us." Thank you for being a part of us!

SOURCES

Bergner, R. M., and A. J. Bridges. 2002. "The Significance of Heavy Pornography Involvement for Romantic Partners: Research and Clinical Implications." *Journal of Sex & Marital Therapy,* 28:193–206.

Blasingame, Gerry D. 2001. "Developmentally Disabled Sexual Offender Rehabilitative Treatment Program Manual and Form." Oklahoma City, OK: Wood 'N' Barnes Publishing.

Brody, Stuart, and Tillman H. C. Kroger. 2006. "The Post-Orgasmic Prolactin Increase Following Intercourse Is Greater Than Following Masturbation and Suggests Greater Satiety." *Biological Psychology,* Vol. 71, no. 3, 312–15.

Conroy, Pat. 2002. *Beach Music.* New York: Dial-Press.

Deaner, Robert O., Amit V. Khera, and Michael L. Platt. 2005. "Monkeys Pay Per View: Adaptive Valuation of Social Images by Rhesus Macaques." *Current Biology,* Vol. 15, no. 6, 543–48.

Dines, Gail. 2010. *Pornland: How Porn Has Hijacked Our Sexuality.* Boston: Beacon Press.

Doherty, William. 1999. "Intentional Marriage: Your Rituals Will Set You Free." Banquet keynote at the annual SmartMarriages Conference, Denver, Colorado. Available at http://www.smartmarriages.com/intentionalmarriage.html.

Felder, L. 2005. "I Gave at the Office." *Psychotherapy Networker,* September/October, accessed online at http://www.psychothera pynetworker.org/.

Gottman, John M., and Robert W. Levenson. 1988. "The Social Psychophysiology of Marriage." In P. Noller & M. A. Fitzpatrick, eds., *Perspectives on Marital Interaction.* Clevedon, England: Multilingual Matters, 182–99.

Karen, Robert. 1990. "Becoming Attached." *The Atlantic Monthly,* February.

Master, Sarah L., Naomi I. Eisenberger, Shelley E. Taylor, Bruce D. Naliboff, David Shirinyan, and Matthew D. Lieberman. 2009. "A Picture's Worth: Partner Photographs Reduce Experimentally Induced Pain." *Psychological Science* 20:1316–18.

Nakken, Craig. 1996. *The Addictive Personality: Understanding the Addictive Process and Compulsive Behavior,* 2nd ed. Center City, MN: Hazelden.

Nouwen, Henri. 2006. *Bread for the Journey: A Daybook of Wisdom and Faith.* New York: HarperOne.

Pollack, William. 1998. *Real Boys.* New York: Henry Holt and Company.

Schwarz, Norbert, and Gerald Clore. 1983. "Mood, Misattribution, and Judgments of Well-Being: Informative and Directive Functions of Affective States." *Journal of Personality and Social Psychology,* 45: 513–23.

Tracy, Lance. *Adult Entertainment: Disrobing an American Idol.* Seattle, WA: CustomFlix.

Tronick, Ed. 2008. "Law and Order Taps Infant-Mother Paradigm Research." *The American Psychoanalyst,* Vol. 42, no. 4, 5.

Wexler, David B. 2009. *Men in Therapy: New Approaches for Effective Treatment.* New York: W. W. Norton and Co.

———. 2010. "Shame-O-Phobias: Why Men Fear Therapy." *Psychotherapy Networker,* May/June, 22.

White, C. 1973. "The Effects of Viewing Films of Different Arousal Content on the Eating Behavior of Obese and Normal Weight Subjects." *Dissertation Abstracts International,* 34 [5-B]:23–24.

Zillman, Dolf, and Jennings Bryant. 1988. "Effects of Prolonged Consumption of Pornography on Family Values." *Journal of Family Issues,* Vol. 9, no. 4, 518–44.

Index

191

About the Authors

Mark Chamberlain, PhD, is a psychologist and clinical director of ARCH, a counseling center in South Jordan and Clearfield, Utah, which provides intensive treatment for individuals and couples healing from pornography and other sexual addictions. He is the author or coauthor of several books, including *Willpower Is Not Enough: Why We Don't Succeed at Change; Confronting Pornography;* and *Wanting More: The Challenge of Enjoyment in the Age of Addiction.* He has been a favorite presenter in cities throughout the United States on the topics of healing addiction and sexuality. He and his wife, Jenny, are the parents of seven children. Website: www.archcounseling.com. Blog: http://markchamberlainphd.blogspot.com

Geoff Steurer, MS, LMFT, is a licensed marriage and family therapist in private practice in St. George, Utah. He is the founder and executive director of LifeSTAR of St. George, a three-phase recovery program for couples and individuals affected by pornography addiction and other sexually compulsive behaviors (www.LifeSTARstgeorge.com). Geoff regularly presents at local and national conferences on topics related to marriage and pornography addiction recovery. He is passionate about providing ongoing education on social media sites and his blog (www .geoffsteurer.com). He completed a bachelor's degree in communications studies from Brigham Young University and a master's degree in marriage and family therapy from Auburn University. He is married to Jody Young Steurer and they are the parents of four children.